GARDEN DESIGN

GARDEN DESIGN

INSPIRATION AND IDEAS

ANDREW MIKOLAJSKI

ROBERT HALE • LONDON

For Finetta

First published in Great Britain 2014

ISBN 978-0-7090-9195-0

Robert Hale Limited
Clerkenwell House
Clerkenwell Green
London EC1R 0HT

www.halebooks.com

A catalogue record for this book is available from the British Library

2 4 6 8 10 9 7 5 3 1

Typeset by Eurodesign
Printed in China

CONTENTS

ACKNOWLEDGEMENTS

This book grew out of a course in garden design that I taught over a number of years at Warwickshire College. As such, I thought it would be easy to write. It wasn't – and it certainly would not have been possible without the help and input of many friends and colleagues. Jackie Herald of The Extra Room read through the text and also supplied many beautiful images and drawings for which I am profoundly grateful. Deborah Hey and Ann Bond also read and made many helpful suggestions on the text. Matt Kinross gave particular attention to the Draughting chapter and I am grateful for his comments and guidance. Francesca Certo supplied additional drawings. My editors at Robert Hale, Alexander Stilwell and Nikki Edwards, were unfailingly polite and patient, and working with them was a real pleasure.

I should say that all opinions expressed here are my own and any errors are solely mine.

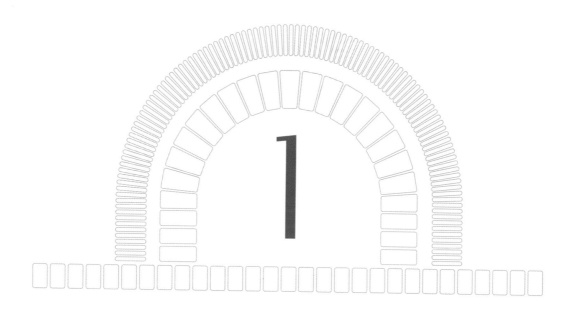

A BRIEF HISTORY OF GARDEN DESIGN

Please don't skip this chapter on the basis that it doesn't sound like a practical chapter. What happened in the past has a huge bearing on what we do in gardens today. But this is a huge subject – and since this has to be brief, I shall be making some sweeping generalizations.

It's useful to know something about garden history not because you should be looking to recreate history in your gardens, but because so many received ideas about how to make gardens have their roots in the past. You may be surprised. And the gardens of the past have much to teach us, if only to reveal how much we take for granted in gardening. Surprisingly often, you will find the answer (or at least *an* answer) to any design conundrum you face in the gardens of the past.

What follows is written from a personal perspective as a designer. Therefore I don't intend to discuss here the gardens of antiquity, medieval gardens or gardens of the Far East, as they do not form part of what I see as an ongoing Western tradition. (So I'm leaving Japanese gardens out of the present discussion – they'll surface elsewhere.) As such, this chapter is Euro-centric by intention.

The further back in time we look (this is also a generalization), the less information we have about gardens, and surviving evidence largely relates to big-scale, big-budget gardens. Before the nineteenth century and the rise of a moneyed middle class, the gardens we know most about are the grand gardens of royalty and the aristocracy. No matter. Many elements of these have filtered down into the gardens of today – more than you would think.

When you survey gardens as we're about to do here, two fundamentals strike you. So much in design depends, firstly, on the prevailing climate and, secondly, on the client's budget. When you look at gardening historically, there's been a steady trend towards low-maintenance solutions, generally out of economic necessity (not only of funds but of time) – though that may also have much to do with redistribution of wealth. High-maintenance gardens are generally intentionally so – they are a conscious display of wealth (and as such are often conceived as public spaces).

Looking at gardens historically also enables us to address (if not precisely answer) that fundamental question – what exactly is a garden for? The great gardens of the past were often created not just as statements of power, but for pleasure (as toys), for relaxation and – rather importantly – for entertaining. In other words, for show. You might invite into your garden people you would never have in the house. Something of that tradition lingers on at royal garden parties, where it's possible for the monarch to entertain a large number of people without actually having to speak to all of them.

I am not suggesting, incidentally, that you approach design as a kind of pastiche – you are not looking to create a pseudo-Renaissance garden, for instance. In any case, whenever you visit a historic garden, you are seeing it as it is today, not as originally created. Trees have a habit of growing and may be much bigger now than they ever were in the imagination of the designer who planted them. Stone and concrete wear away, discolour and gather moss – all part of the garden's life. There's actually an important lesson here: whenever you make a garden, you have to have an eye on its future – how will it look five, ten, even twenty years down the road?

It also has to be said that only a certain amount can be learnt from looking at photographs of historic gardens, still less from looking at plans. To appreciate a garden, you need to be in it. Often, the overall effect depends on the manipulation of the space, the proportions and views beyond and upwards to the sky (more on this in Chapter 3) – also, on the pace of the garden, the expectation of the speed at which you will move through the spaces and where you will pause.

Three major styles

Speaking broadly – very broadly – I identify three major styles of gardening, looked at historically: Italian Renaissance, English landscape, and Islamic. Underlying this is my firm conviction – a sweeping generalization, I admit – that the whole of Western culture pretty much has its roots in Renaissance Italy. It's no coincidence that the great Italian bankers were the first people who seemingly had money to burn. Although the following discusses gardens made on the grandest of scales, the principles of good garden design remain the same. Many elements can be translated into more modest schemes.

When lecturing on garden history, I am occasionally asked about medieval and monastery gardens and why I always exclude these from my survey. The short answer is that they do not, as I see it, form part of a continuing tradition of garden-making. The slightly longer answer warrants a digression.

Apart from being flowery places to sit and woo a loved one – as suggested by troubadours and *trouvères** – gardens of the Middle Ages had a practical function: the growing of medicinal herbs. Interestingly, a great many of these plants, plus the knowledge of how to use them, was brought into the West by returning Crusaders who would stop for refreshment at monasteries, which also functioned as hospitals and hospices. Along with the plants came smatterings of Islamic culture, including how to lay out the garden itself.

ITALIAN RENAISSANCE

As a typical example of the Italian style, take the Villa d'Este – the palace built for Ippolito II d'Este at Tivoli, near Rome, in the sixteenth century. What is immediately striking about this garden (and others of its type) are the straight lines and the reliance on symmetry and focal points. Second, you might note the high quality of the hard landscaping – beautiful balustrades, porticos, statues and fountains. Such gardens were not built on the cheap. As a response to the climate – lots of clear, sunny and even bakingly hot days – this is a garden made to create shade, with tall, mainly evergreen trees and hedges and plenty of water to cool the air – canals, pools, fountains and cascades. There's little, if any, reliance on flowers. In hot conditions, flowers are transitory, and their colours would fade rapidly.

Another important – in fact, highly significant – element of these Italian Renaissance gardens is the view on to the landscape beyond. You might even say that this is rather the point of these gardens – appreciative as you may be of particular aspects of the design while you are in it, you are also impelled to look beyond it. While on one level you could say that the essence of an Italian garden is a strict use of geometry (and this is evident from the plans), at a deeper level is the tension between that geometry and the landscape beyond – the managed space of the garden versus the uncontrolled (and uncontrollable) one beyond it. This is something that you can really only understand when you are present in the garden itself – a conflict between the highly managed structures of the garden and the natural world. Slightly counter-intuitively (and this also creates tension), the views on to the outside landscape also convey the very real sense that the garden itself is unbounded, endless in fact. You inevitably feel you are being pulled out into the world beyond as your eye constantly flicks towards it. An interesting case is the Boboli garden, which gives a view on to the city of Florence – the clear implication being that the townscape somehow 'belongs' to the garden.

In an important sense, therefore, an Italian garden is not enclosed (even though there may be separate enclosures within it) – it is fundamentally created to look outwards.

*They were not 'wandering minstrels', but usually aristocrats with a high level of education.

Spirit of america/Shutterstock.com

A typical Italian garden has a central main axis that runs from a main door of the house with secondary axes at right angles that end in small enclosures

Another principal feature of this type of garden is a main, central axis, generally running from the public door of the house and open at its furthest end – this may form a promontory or platform from which to survey the landscape, as at Boboli, in Florence. Joining this central axis at right angles are several secondary axes that lead off towards little enclosures, usually shady retreats – plantings of evergreens or artificial grottoes with benches, fountains and statues. The axis may be marked by a statue, bench or fountain, a focal point that draws the eye to it – hence you feel drawn to go there.

These too have a further significance, and this is something the modern visitor may not immediately be aware of – the grottoes that close the secondary axes are hidden from the general view, making perfect hideaways. They are ideal, therefore, for an amorous tryst. Furthermore, the frequent narrowing of the path as you reach the destination is not simply a visual canard calculated to make the path seem longer than it is (uses of false perspective are discussed elsewhere), but forces a couple to move closer to one another as they reach their goal – particularly if the lady is wearing a big court dress. Before long, you would find shoulders and upper arms touching. Leaving aside the *giocchi d'acqua* – where, at the touch of a button, guests would be drenched with water (which wouldn't make me laugh) – in an important sense, a Renaissance garden has a playful, even sexy, quality.

That quality of playfulness is also to be found in the labyrinth or maze, also a regular feature of these gardens – great places for chasing your lover in the dusk. Maybe here we can also recognize that very strong desire to lose oneself in a garden – and not necessarily in a good way: a maze is playful only up to a point. The feeling of being lost is potentially an unpleasant one. (There's more tension there – at what point does delicious play tip over into genuine danger?)

When Catherine de' Medici moved to France as the bride of Henry II in the first part of the sixteenth century, she took Italian culture, and an awful lot of money, with her – including this style of garden-making (as well as Italian cuisine, painting and music). So you'll find the ultimate example of the Italianate garden not in Italy but in France, specifically at Louis XIV's chateau at Versailles, the garden of which was laid out from around 1660 by the master landscape architect André le Notre. Le Notre's masterpiece, however, is generally considered to be the garden at Vaux-le-Vicomte, created for Nicolas Fouquet a few years after this. A couple of things are of note – apart from a main axis that apparently extends to infinity, there is cunning use of water (which also seems to pull the heavens downward to ground level). From the house, the main canal is hidden by the fall of the land. As you process through the space, it suddenly – and dramatically – comes into view. This is a garden that's less about plants than about the manipulation of perspective. But again – you need to be there to appreciate it.

Grand as they are, both Vaux and Versailles were built (I use the word advisedly) not only for display but as spaces for entertainment, for parties on the biggest scale – they functioned as a backdrop to other events. But Versailles had an additional function – to underline Louis XIV's status as absolute ruler. As such, it has a kind of austerity. The playful quality that characterizes Italian models is less in evidence.

ENGLISH LANDSCAPE

The French style (as it had become, though manifestly grounded in Italian models) was copied throughout continental Europe, which even today is peppered with mini-Versailles palaces (some not so mini), all with their matching gardens. The outstanding example in Britain (where you don't find so many, for reasons that are about to become apparent) is the William and Mary garden at Hampton Court, laid out around the turn of the eighteenth century.

But for all the vogue for things Italian in the England of the seventeenth and eighteenth centuries – young men embarking on the Grand Tour brought back Italian style in architecture and gardening as well as works of art, music and syphilis – this was never a style that was likely to have a lasting appeal in Britain. Too showy, too contrived, too *foreign*.

Such gardens are high-maintenance – intentionally. Fountains had to be pumped, hedges clipped, and gravel paths kept weed-free. You can't have a garden like this without money to spend. In the eighteenth century in England, there was something of a backlash to all this artifice. The South Sea Bubble, the crash in the stock market that occurred around 1720, may well have accelerated its demise – many members of the aristocracy found themselves bankrupt or very nearly so. Besides, who needs a garden of tall hedges, fountains and shady walkways in a cool, predominantly damp climate?

Painshill is a classic English 'park', laid out in the eighteenth century, with stretches of water and eyecatchers such as the Gothic temple shown here

The English landscape garden, therefore, represents something of a response to more limited resources. Typically – the garden at Stowe in Buckinghamshire is a familiar example – it comprises an open parkland of undulating hills and panoramas, lakes and stands of trees, all designed to look as natural as possible. It may also not be too fanciful to suggest that the relative freedom of these landscapes is a celebration of a national sense of liberty and rejection of despotism. Italian elements never went away, however – expect to come across temples, arches, pavilions and statues, generally in a neoclassical style.

But is an English landscape garden as natural as all that? Geometry – in terms of shapes and volumes and how they relate to one another – is actually highly important. Furthermore, an English landscape has the quality of a stage-set and many examples were created to be viewed from the north. As the sun crosses the heavens, various features are illuminated at specific times of day. Instead of the focal point, there is the eyecatcher – an obelisk, a classical temple, maybe even a stand of trees – which is suddenly bathed in sunlight. And those lakes? Often the sides are disguised with planting, so, as also at Versailles, incidentally, your impression is that the water stretches on forever. In short, an English garden is as contrived, in its way, as a Renaissance one. And an English landscape is expensive in the making, involving much moving of the earth, transplanting of mature trees, and diversion of water. It's only once that it's up and running that maintenance costs all but disappear.

There's a tantalizing (because so brief) reference to one in Jane Austen's *Pride and Prejudice*, when her aunt and uncle take Elizabeth on a tour of Pemberley, Mr Darcy's country seat:

> The park was very large, and contained great variety of ground. They entered it in one of its lowest points, and drove for some time through a beautiful wood stretching over a wide extent.
>
> Elizabeth's mind was too full for conversation, but she saw and admired every remarkable spot and point of view. They gradually ascended for half-a-mile, and then found themselves at the top of a considerable eminence, where the wood ceased, and the eye was instantly caught by Pemberley House, situated on the opposite side of a valley, into which the road with some abruptness wound. It was a large, handsome stone building, standing well on rising ground, and backed by a ridge of high woody hills; and in front, a stream of some natural importance was swelled into greater, but without any artificial appearance. Its banks were neither formal nor falsely adorned. Elizabeth was delighted. She had never seen a place for which nature had done more, or where natural beauty had been so little counteracted by an awkward taste. They were all of them warm in their admiration; and at that moment she felt that to be mistress of Pemberley might be something!

This style then swept Europe, especially Germany, as part of the vogue for all things British in the late eighteenth and early nineteenth century. There's quite a description of the making of one in Goethe's *Elective Affinities* (and in Jean-Jacques Rousseau's *La Nouvelle Héloise*). After the self-imposed constraints of earlier times, there came a desire to get back to nature (but you can never tell with Goethe – he may have been being ironic). It was probably around this time that the English began to gain the reputation of being great garden-makers – an idea that persists to this day. The term 'English garden' really refers specifically to this style, but is nowadays probably used more freely just to designate 'the gardens of England'.

The English landscape garden became tied up with the idea of the 'picturesque'. Such a scene as Jane Austen describes might be enlivened with ruins, generally of artificial construction, possibly even populated by 'ruined' people – an unwashed, unshaven hermit might be required to live on site.

Just as in Italian and French gardens, however, the English landscape barely involves flowers, interest in which came later. These are still gardens of the wealthy, calculated to manipulate and control the landscape. Whether in an obvious or subtle way, the effect is the same.

ISLAMIC

'The gardens of Islam' is a phrase that carries as much resonance as 'the English garden'. You could say that the notion of a garden is even more deeply ingrained in Islamic culture than it is in the West – an Islamic garden seems to hold deep symbolism within it, and Islamic art is founded on plant motifs, seen everywhere in its architecture, on carpets and other textiles and ceramics. Western art has been more concerned with the human form.

On the face of it, the Islamic garden embodies the exact opposite of the two Western European styles already discussed. Far from being a public space, where anyone could wander around, an Islamic garden is fundamentally private, and, to create privacy, is always enclosed – it offers a retreat from the world, rather than being emphatically in it.

Traditionally, an Islamic garden is geometric in design, typically a square or rectangle, and strictly divided into four by straight water rills – just as the universe was cut by four great rivers (Pison, Gihon, Hiddekel and the Euphrates). At the centre where they meet is a tank of water – circular, square or rectangular – symbolizing the meeting of God and man, and to one side (usually) a portico with seating.

So far, therefore, no plants. In fact, the plants may be incidental for, as with the Italian gardens, the overriding concern is to create shade and to cool the air further with running water. This lack of plants dismayed – initially – no less a gardener than Vita Sackville-West (more on her later), who travelled to Persia in 1926 with high hopes of these fabled gardens. She rapidly came to a different conclusion. As she wrote in *Passenger to Teheran*:

Imagine you have ridden in summer for four days across a plain…and for days, even weeks, you must ride with no shade, and the sun overhead…Then, when you come to trees and running water, you will call it a garden. It will not be flowers and their garishness that your eyes crave for, but a green cavern full of shadows and pools where goldfish dart, and the sound of a little stream.

One of the most familiar of all Islamic gardens is that of the Alhambra, the Moorish palace complex in Granada, Spain. Here, the scheme comprises shady courtyards, pools, canals and fountains with only a few hedges and palm trees providing the green material. How the elements of this style became assimilated into Western gardens would make a fascinating study.

The usual story is that the Moors brought the style through Spain (and southern Italy) from the eleventh century. But it's also true that the Crusaders brought back many plants (mainly medicinal) from the Middle East during the same period. These found their way into monasteries, where, as I have mentioned, the Crusaders would have been offered hospitality, often literally, in the sense that monasteries had important functions as hospitals and hospices. Monastery gardens, curiously, are frequently laid out on Islamic (or, at least, geometric) principles, often enclosed and functioning as places of retreat, with covered cloisters that make shady walking places.

There's one other, easily overlooked aspect of an Islamic garden, and that is the intimate relationship between the garden and the building. The stretches of water are often placed so as to reflect the building.

Victorian England

It's only in the nineteenth century and with the post-Industrial Revolution rise of a moneyed middle class that you see the development of gardens that most of us can relate to more easily. A hugely influential figure was William Robinson (1838–1935) – he is much less well remembered than his colleague and contemporary Gertrude Jekyll, but is at least as important. Many of our ideas about gardens can be traced back to him, and seem strikingly modern. And it's him that we have to thank for the invention of 'cottage gardens' – supposedly a vernacular style that has parallels in the Arts and Crafts movement with its emphasis on traditional crafts and simplicity. In his use of native plants, Robinson was also an environmentalist *avant la lettre*.

If he seems radical today, that may be because he was reacting against a trend that had become common in gardens of his time – namely, 'gardenesque'. John Claudius Loudon (1783–1843), botanist and cemetery designer and one of the perpetrators of this style, was concerned that gardens were becoming *too* natural and should be more conspicuously man-made. He was a great advocate of symmetry in a design (with a correspondingly definite axis). This is the era of carpet bedding – formally designed beds planted with exotic incomers (frequently half-hardy annuals) and often including yuccas as accent plants. Trees – the exotic monkey puzzle (*Araucaria araucana*) was particularly popular – were planted in solitary splendour as specimens in lawns to be admired from all sides. Victorian parterres – which still survive in some stately homes and public gardens – are often strikingly reminiscent of Italian gardens of a few centuries before.

Robinson was trenchant in his views, and fiercely rejected the artificiality of the gardenesque and topiary. The typical 'English' garden of today, as made by such plant lovers as join gardening clubs and visit RHS flower shows, probably owes more to him – and almost certainly unwittingly – than to any other gardener of the past. It's to him we owe the idea of using mainly hardy perennials planted in natural-looking drifts as ground cover. Also, his is the convention of laying out the garden that immediately joins the house in a formal, even geometric style, then allowing more informality the further you go away from the house. He pretty much invented 'wild gardening', by which he understood the use of hardy perennials planted in woodland, by water or to simulate a meadow. In essence, his approach is untidy and relaxed.

This brings me to Gertrude Jekyll, surely one of the most misrepresented of all gardeners of the past. Nowadays, she is remembered chiefly for the Jekyllean border (if ever anyone suggests making one – talk them out of it). This is the grand border of considerable length, composed mainly of perennials, that is planned for summer colour: grey foliage at each end; then blue, pale yellow, white and pale pink; stronger yellow through to orange and red (this at the centre of the border); then the inverse of the preceding, with orange and deep yellow giving way to paler yellow, with white and pale pink; but ending with purple and lilac rather than blue. For good reason, she has sometimes been criticized for applying to gardening colour principles more appropriate to interior design.

But she created these borders mainly for clients who spent most of their time in London, retreating to their country house in the summer, when, for a six- to eight-week period, the herbaceous border had to look stunning. In order to achieve this, it's necessary to have a dedicated nursery area, where plants (and potential replacements) can be grown on. An army of gardeners would plant the bed in anticipation of their employers' arrival, then would have their work cut out staking the plants, dead-heading them, then, as they went over, replacing them with others (held in reserve in the nursery). At the end of the summer, the border could be cleared and left as an empty plot until the following year. It simply isn't practical to do this in this day and age, not only because of the space and labour required but because we expect our gardens to contain something of interest for most of the year.

Besides – just how good did these borders look, anyway? Miss Jekyll, who trained as a painter, was famously short-sighted, and what she saw was a Monet-like wash of colour. When we look at one of Monet's paintings of his garden, we are seeing it literally through his eyes. For anyone with normal vision, the same isn't true of a Jekyll planting. Apart from the grand border, outlined above, she was also keen on single-colour plantings. In a blue garden, however, she would often include touches of white or yellow.

Such schemes smack of painterly contrivance. But her more workable ideas are overlooked – for instance, the idea of a nuttery carpeted in spring with primulas. This is more than just a 'picture' – it was a conscious reference back to the (possibly imaginary) past (in the spirit of the Arts and Crafts movement), when hazel was an important economic plant, grown for nuts for eating and stems for basketry and fence-making. She did also come up with another very intriguing idea – that the garden should curtsey to the house.

The twentieth century and beyond

Two influential gardens stand out, both made in the mid-twentieth century – Hidcote Manor Garden and Sissinghurst, both now managed by the National Trust. These gardens were much written about and continue to attract plenty of visitors – though it is impossible for us to see them now as their creators intended. But they embody so many garden trends that are obstinately persistent.

The striking thing about both of these large gardens is that they are laid out as a series of 'rooms' – it's become something of a mantra of garden design that the best way to deal with a large site (and even sometimes a small one) is to partition it in similar fashion. 'Doorways' in walls and hedges lead from one enclosure to the next. Perhaps. If nothing else, Sissinghurst offers a brilliant solution to how to design a successful scheme within the limitations imposed by the site – in this case, the ruined walls of the former castle. The credit for this lies not with Vita Sackville-West (1892–1962) but with her husband, the somewhat overshadowed Harold Nicolson (1886–1968). Vita's style of planting became hugely influential, largely because of her weekly gardening column in the *Observer*, and is still very much present in much of garden-making today – the idea of a relaxed, 'mixed' planting (shrubs, perennials and bulbs, possibly with a few annuals) within a fairly formalized structure.

But what's generally overlooked is that the whole point of planning a garden as a series of rooms is the allowance it makes for seasonal planting. An area planted with early bulbs and spring-flowering shrubs might delight early on in the year, but be deadly dull for the rest of it. If these are given a room of their own, you need not set foot there again until the following year. A case in point is the lime walk at Sissinghurst, an avenue of pleached limes (*Tilia*), each one of which is underplanted with spring bulbs – a treat when they are all in flower and the bare horizontally trained stems of the limes are glowing with fresh green leaf buds. (Interestingly, this strictly controlled planting leads to a much more informal nuttery.) In summer, it is simply a shady walkway, probably hardly visited.

These gardens also have the potential for drama in that so much is hidden from immediate view – each new room has the potential of offering a new discovery (something that can be achieved even in a small garden). At Hidcote, made by the American Lawrence Johnston (1871–1958), an area of note comprises little more than a hedged enclosure that wraps around a central circular tank of water. After so much rich planting elsewhere in the garden, this reads as a place of great tranquillity, especially on a hot day.

One important gardener of the following generation who is frequently overlooked is Alan Bloom (1906–2005) – perhaps because his impact has been greatest on suburban gardens (which are generally not celebrated). Yet the odd thing is that other influential writers such as Beth Chatto and Rosemary Verey are at one in saying what a beautiful garden he created at Bressingham in Norfolk. More than any garden-maker mentioned so far, he recognized the need for hardy, low-maintenance plants – because he always had the gardener with limited leisure time in mind. He owed much to German gardens, from which he imported many plants (often readily identifiable by their German names). He is chiefly remembered now for inventing the island bed – usually roughly oval or kidney-shaped and planted with a mix of tough plants that look good over a long period. Frequently these were conifers, heathers and grasses, with a few notable perennials. Unfortunately, the island bed became something of a cliché of suburban gardens and an essential element has been forgotten. This is a splendid way of planting a large, irregular, sloping site. The idea is that you should be able to look over the plants, then take a meandering path through them. Paths, by the way, are broad and grassed – in fact, to be practical, a grass path *has* to be broad (more on this in Chapter 6).

Something similar – also conceived for low maintenance – is discernible in the work of Dutch plantsman and designer Piet Oudolf (born in 1944), to whom we owe prairie planting. The point of this style is to grow in close proximity certain tough, hardy perennials, generally late-flowering. Packed together, they need no staking and grow to a similar height. The plants are arranged in interlocking drifts and ideally follow the lie of a sloping site, so from the top you look over them. Prairie planting was really created to meet the needs of garden-making in a harsh climate. The colour range is essentially muted – dull pinks, mauves, rust reds, with maybe some warmer oranges and yellows – along with quite a lot of beige from the grasses and seed-heads from earlier-flowering plants. Christopher Lloyd (1921–2006), who created a famous, post-Jekyllean garden at Great Dixter, East Sussex, allegedly hated it.

A prairie planting has its moment in November – caught in the cold morning light with a riming of frost and rising from a skirt of fog (conditions, incidentally, that are more likely to be met in Holland, Germany and other parts of northern Europe, and less so in a balmier climate such as the UK's).

Sustainable gardening

Sustainability has become the buzzword of modern garden-making – and I have puzzled for some time about what it actually means. It implies that the making of a garden should have the minimum impact on the environment, with a corresponding reduction of the carbon footprint. In practical terms, this means not making radical changes to a site, and instead working with what's there. It often also involves using local materials, possibly reclaimed materials. I'm no eco-warrior, but often this makes economic sense.

Louis XIV's garden, therefore, represents the antithesis of sustainability, as it was made on a swamp that had to be drained before any work could begin. The vast earthworks involved in making both Renaissance gardens and English landscape gardens, and the transportation of hard landscaping materials (often from Italy, if marble), make these very much gardens of the past.

Nevertheless, I find I can take this idea only so far. Good gardening involves – and always has involved – the destruction of the environment to some extent. Historically – and even today – that legacy gives pause for thought.

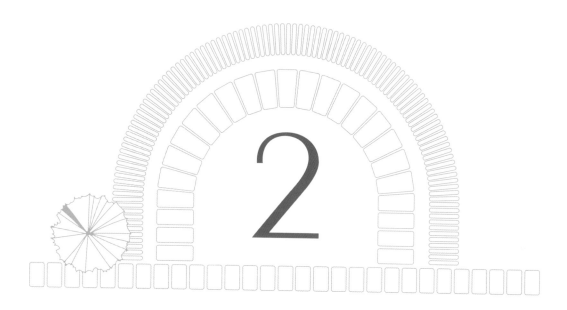

ASSESSING THE SITE

Site assessment is one of the designer's most important skills – you need to be able to walk into any garden and rapidly make up your mind about the options and the kind of garden you will be able to make. Obviously this is important when you are buying a new property, even more so if you are designing professionally. In the latter case, a client will most probably have no ideas, or have some ideas that can immediately be recognized as impractical. If there is anything that impresses clients, it's a designer's ability to take in a site at a glance and point out its possibilities within minutes of meeting them – especially if you can do this in the middle of winter (when designers are often commissioned), when the ground is largely bare and the weather may be overcast. Clients themselves may be new to the area or may have already made some attempts to design the garden themselves with limited success. If it is your own garden you are working on, adequate site assessment can avoid costly mistakes later.

Site assessment has little to do with your aesthetic sense and almost everything to do with practicalities. Leaving aside budgetary constraints, the potential of every site is always strictly limited. In practice, this simplifies matters greatly – it reduces the number of alternative solutions available to you. Depending on the property, the site may be bare or may already be planted. If the latter, there may be valuable clues as to soil type. A good assessment of the site will guide your choice of hard landscaping. You also need to consider the impact your own plans will make

This lawn is in very poor condition and the Leylandii conifers at the boundary have never been properly controlled.

on the space in practical terms – not only as regards what you are going to create but what you are going to get rid of. Felling a ghastly overgrown conifer may let light into a garden, but may also expose an equally ghastly view.

Pay some attention to what is outside the garden, things over which you have no control – other buildings, telegraph poles, large trees, etc. You will either have to think about screening these with plant material or fencing or mitigating their impact in some way, perhaps by careful use of focal points in the design (see Chapter 3).

LocaL climate

The climate has a huge influence on the type of garden you make – and this is as true today as it's ever been. And climate is a factor over which you have no control. When fashion designer Yves Saint-Laurent took on the Majorelle garden in Marrakech in 1980 he painted the walls an intense blue – a design 'statement' that was widely copied by others in the following years (including at the Chelsea Flower Show). But such saturated colours work best in strong sunlight and do not transfer easily to northerly, damper areas where skies are often grey and overcast.

If you've lived in the property for some time (or are working professionally on a garden close to home), you'll already be familiar with the local climate. But you may have moved to a new property in an unfamiliar location or be taking on a project some distance from home. Just thinking of the UK, most people are aware of the north–south divide – obviously it's colder up north than down south. Spring arrives later in the north, and winter sooner. In the west, it tends to be mild, damp and warm. Conversely, the east of the country is cold and dry.

Coastal sites have their own issues, the principal of which is salty sea breezes. Not many plants like these. By the sea, it's always a degree or so cooler in summer than inland and, in winter, a degree or so warmer. Frosts can be quite rare, in fact, so you can grow plants that wouldn't survive inland. For an accurate summary, refer to the local meteorological station, as these are not hard and fast rules. Depending on the lie of the land and prevailing winds, the climate can vary significantly even within a ten-mile radius.

Orientation and aspect

This is the direction in which the garden is facing or, put another way, which parts are lit by the sun (and therefore warmed) at particular times of day – and which will be in the shade. This will certainly help guide your plant choice and also give you some clues about the design itself. You do not need to arm yourself with a compass – just ask yourself (or the client) where the sun sets (which establishes the west) and work back from there. If the sun is shining you'll be able to identify east from west depending on whether it's morning or afternoon. However, while it's possible to bring shelter and shade to an otherwise open and predominantly sunny site, it's usually impossible to do the reverse. A city garden shaded by neighbouring buildings is going to stay shady. It's generally possible to make some snap judgements straight away – you won't, for instance, be able to make a successful kitchen garden in a predominantly shady site or a very windy one. Most vegetables, fruiting plants and herbs need to be grown in a sunny, sheltered site. Within a garden, walls, fences and hedges (and to some extent dips and hollows) provide 'microclimates' – small patches where the temperature is warmer or cooler than in the open garden, where there may be shelter from wind or even increased exposure to it. You either have to deal with these microclimates, accept them or, ideally, exploit them.

A sunny wall can present unexpected opportunities for planting. (By sunny I mean facing south or west.) Brick and stone, especially if pale in colour, not only reflect light but absorb heat, staying warm even when the sun is no longer on them. This has a significant effect on woody plants grown against or near walls. The additional heat provided by the wall toughens the wood of shrubs and climbers, often improving flowering and generally increasing tolerance of freezing weather in winter. Unusual and exotic plants that would not be hardy elsewhere in the garden suddenly become options. This is the ideal site for a peach, fig or apricot, or, if that's considered too much work, a less than hardy shrub such as a ceanothus, fremontodendron or callistemon (hardy and shade-tolerant plants such as ivies and pyracanthas have their uses against walls, but

Jackie Herald

The sunny wall offers plenty of scope for growing tender plants. Provided there is no Tree Preservation Order on it, the overgrown sycamore, which casts heavy shade, is best removed.

not here). I'd caution restraint, however, as there is no law that says a wall has to have a plant against it. Some old brick or stone walls are intrinsically beautiful. Why not let them speak, unadorned? Or perhaps put a deciduous plant over them, so you can appreciate them in winter.

A wall facing east or north presents other possibilities. An east-facing wall will not heat up significantly, as the first half of the day is much cooler than the second. A north-facing wall will see hardly any sun at all. Cool aspects suit many climbing plants, which by their very nature are woodlanders, so are adapted to shady conditions. These decisions in themselves may provide guidance for other planting in the vicinity.

Alternatively, the wall may provide shelter for a sitting area – a cool place as a retreat in summer or a warm one for enjoying winter sun.

RAIN SHADOW

If you've ever pressed your back against a wall to shelter from a shower of rain, you'll have ready understanding of this term. Unless the wind is blowing rain directly towards the wall, the soil at the base of it (if there is any) will always be drier than that elsewhere in the garden. If you do introduce plants to ascend a wall, they will have to be kept well-watered during the initial period if they are to establish properly. Dryness at the roots may well continue to be a problem, but plants that like it hot and dry above ground (such as Californian ceanothus and fremontoden-dron) often tolerate dry soil at the roots.

Light and shade

Light levels in a garden vary throughout the year. It sounds obvious, but it's really easy to over-look this if you're assessing a site on a dull day in winter, and it can significantly influence how you plan the space. You need to be able to project ahead and think about light levels at different times of the year. A courtyard that's shaded in winter may well turn out to be a suntrap in summer. Conversely, deciduous trees that are airy when bare, filtering the winter sun and casting intriguing shadows, may well develop a leaden canopy in summer, blocking out all the sunlight. A clue here will be the state of any vegetation, particularly grass, around the base of the trunk. A thin and starved look suggests lack of light and water in summer. Turn that to your advantage – a seat under a deciduous tree may offer an ideal vantage point to survey a planting of late winter bulbs on a mild day, then become a welcome cool retreat on a hot day in summer.

Elements of your own design can also affect light levels. A fence that may be necessary to create privacy will also cast shade. Being more proactive, you can fell or reduce trees to allow more light into a space and you can lighten dark areas by introducing pale colours – painting walls and fences white or using light-coloured hard landscaping materials. In a suntrap garden, you may need to think about creating temporary shade in summer with the use of canopies or other screening – provided there is space in a garage, shed or outbuilding to store these in winter.

Be aware also of the possible impact of your decisions on any neighbouring gardens – a tree or hedge that you plant in your garden to create shelter may well spoil a neighbour's view or cast unwelcome shade in their garden at particular times. It's tempting but often unwise to plant trees on the boundaries, either as screening or so as not to lose too much space within the garden.

Note that soils dry out rapidly in full sun, and much more slowly in shade.

Topography

This grand term means nothing more than the lie of the land – many sites, especially smaller ones, are flat, but you may well be confronted by slopes, dips and hollows, which have to be taken into account. One of the mantras of garden design (though there's some sense in this one) is that a sloping, or uneven, site is intrinsically more dramatic than a flat one (which is considered more 'restful').

Dramatic? Possibly more interesting or, from the designer's perspective, more challenging (and rewarding). A sloping site has to be 'negotiated', managed – or, put more positively, exploited. Even a gently sloping site conveys some sense of discomfort. Any part of the garden that you intend to use for seating and entertaining should really be flat. Gravity alone creates a sense of 'pull' towards the bottom of a slope. The intrinsic contrast between even a gentle slope and a flat area gives the garden a very tangible dynamic.

A garden that slopes away from the house puts the house on a pedestal, as it were, genuinely appearing to curtsey to it in the Jekyllean sense. A slope down towards the house will seem to shelter the area next to the house (usually a patio), making this a very private spot. An unevenly sloping site is 'dynamic' in that you have to vary your pace to traverse it. A flat site has no change of pace, unless you introduce one. A sloping, or uneven, site is one of the few that naturally lends itself to the use of decking. A series of decks always looks elegant, with each new tier serving as a landing stage, or possibly somewhere to relax and take in the view.

Unless money is no object, it's always easiest to deal with the site as it is. Flattening a site, or doing anything major, involves the use (and cost) of earth-moving equipment and the disposal of the spoil which will probably involve the use of skips. If the earth must move for you, the way to keep costs down is to move it somewhere else in the garden. However, if your excavations extend below the topsoil (see p. 27), you must be careful to separate topsoil and subsoil so the two do not get mixed.

There's one other issue with sloping ground, and it concerns perspective. There is always the potential for drama for the following reason – at a glance, it can be difficult to judge the overall area of the site, especially if the slope is steep or varies. This is a matter of simple geometry. Standing at the top of the slope and looking directly ahead, you will form an instant impression of the length of the garden. As you descend the slope, you'll be walking the longer side of the triangle and the boundary will appear to recede from you. (For more on perspective and how to exploit a slope, see Chapter 3.)

If you are going to do anything that involves moving quantities of earth, from a budgetary point of view try to come up with a solution that utilizes all the spoil – so that you do not have to skip valuable topsoil (and subsoil). Costs are involved, not only in skip hire but if you are employing a contractor to do this part of the job, in physically barrowing the excavated earth to the skip. By all means make mounds, raised areas and sunken ones, but keep your eye on how simple it is to do this.

FROST POCKETS

An understanding of these requires some knowledge of the laws of physics. Cold air sinks, as you'll appreciate if you've ever observed a blanket of fog rolling atmospherically over moorland. On a cold night, frost will collect in any dips in the garden, even if they are halfway down a slope. A hollow in the ground that presents as a potential suntrap in summer can become a death trap for vulnerable plants in winter. There's always a frost pocket where a slope meets a wall.

Frost pockets are a fact of life and have to be managed (with appropriate use and choice of plant material) rather than necessarily solved. If you do move earth around – or build walls – be aware that you may be inadvertently creating cold spots. If you are planting hedging on a sloping site, the solution is easy. Trim the hedge so that the lower parts of the stems are clear, then any frost will roll through them and on down the slope.

WINDY SITES

Open, exposed sites present particular challenges, regardless of whether they are flat or sloping. Wind is the enemy of nearly all plants, affecting not only the shapes they make but the rate at which they grow – it has a dwarfing effect, and otherwise tall-growing trees and shrubs develop as bent and scrubby. And windy gardens are seldom pleasant places in which to sit and relax. Conversely, exposed sites on the sides of hills often have spectacular views, rather in the manner of an English landscape. Here your best bet may be to devise some low-level planting that will appear to flow into the landscape, perhaps with a few sheltered plat-

A garden with different levels is always an exciting project – but with pitfalls. Check whether the foot of the wall creates a frost pocket, for instance.

forms from which to enjoy the view. Erecting solid fences and planting thick hedges can sometimes be counterproductive – they will serve only to increase turbulence within a site rather than filtering the wind. (For more details, see Chapter 8.)

Even small, apparently sheltered gardens can have windy patches. The narrow passage that is often to one side of a semi-detached house can act as a wind funnel, creating a draught at the garden end. Either filter this with trellis or light planting or choose plants that will tolerate buffeting.

VERY SMALL GARDENS

A few gardens present the opposite problem. A confined space, such as might be attached to a basement, can be practically airless, as tall surrounding walls restrict air movement. They are usually dank. Grass is not a viable option – not only will it not grow well if light and rainfall are in short supply, but there may well be no room to store a lawnmower. Paving or decking (or synthetic grass) is the best solution. And while walls can be painted white, to reflect what light there is, I am less keen on using mirrors to 'expand' the space, or trompe l'oeil paintings of hypothetical landscapes or dummy doors attached to walls (which are meant to give the impression that they open on to another, much larger space beyond). A more effective solution is to confront the problem head-on and think counter-intuitively. A few very large containers, lavishly planted, give a sense of opulence in even the smallest space. And while I am generally no fan of hanging baskets, walls can support a range of containers that, filled with trailing plants, can create a lush, tropical look. Enclosed gardens make no reference to a landscape or, often, any specific geographic location.

A small garden on a modern housing development may well be overlooked by neighbouring gardens and it may not be practical – or kind to the neighbours – to erect a tall fence. Consider marking off the garden from its neighbours aesthetically – perhaps by imposing a strictly geometric design if the others are more informal or by creating a wildflower meadow and pond if the others are neatly manicured (for types of low hedges and fences, see Chapter 8).

The soil

Garden soil is fascinating. You don't need a degree in soil science, or even to carry out any detailed soil analysis, but you need to be able to make judgements about the condition of the soil in the garden – and whether it needs any improvement before planting. The type of soil can guide your plant choice – and hence your design – as much as any of the factors discussed above.

But ask even experienced gardeners what their soil is like and watch a look of panic appear on their faces (no one likes to have an area of ignorance exposed, so, if you are doing this professionally, the question is often better left unasked). Small wonder, actually, as there are two, completely unrelated, issues to deal with when assessing the soil – pH and texture – with both having an impact on what you can grow, but one being more fixable than the other. While it's relatively straightforward to judge texture, you cannot determine the pH of soil just by looking at it.

SOIL PH

Soils are either acid or alkaline, or occasionally neutral, as measured on the pH scale. As you learnt in school, this runs from 0 to 14, with 7 being neutral. Lower numbers are acid, higher ones are alkaline. The good news is that most plants cannot tell the difference and are equally at home in either. But some definitely can, and it's these you need to be concerned with. (Most soils, incidentally, are slightly acid, with a pH of around 5.5 or above.) You only need to worry if you, or a client, want to grow acid-loving (or lime-hating) plants. Acid soils are sometimes sandy and/or peaty, and alkaline (or limey) soils are sometimes chalky (with gobbets of white chalk in them). While heavy clay soils tend towards the alkaline, this cannot be assumed. In practice, the texture of the soil offers few clues at all – it's possible for pockets of acid soil to overlie chalk and vice versa.

Consulting a geological map can help. I wouldn't bother with soil-testing kits, which often yield ambiguous results (besides, you only ever test a teaspoon of soil) – still less the electronic ones, with a needle that you plunge into the ground: these are simply not accurate. By far the best approach is snooping. If you're in a rural situation with outcrops of limestone in the landscape, the ground will probably be alkaline (though always with the possibility of acid patches). If you are gazing over sweeps of heather, conditions are probably acid. In a built-up area, have a look at what seems to be thriving in neighbouring gardens. If you see a lot of rhododendrons, camellias and heathers, the soil is almost certainly acid; if there are ivies, elders and clematis everywhere, assume it is alkaline.

A suck-it-and-see approach is often the best guide – an acid-loving plant such as a rhododendron will soon look sickly and turn yellow in unsuitable conditions.

It is not worth trying to change the pH of a site. It's possible to raise the pH by adding lime – but this persists in the soil for many years. And while you can acidify alkaline soil, the lime soon takes over – repeated applications of the acidifying agent are necessary. You might try raised beds (see Chapter 8), but even here I'd be cautious. Acid-loving plants simply fail to integrate in a garden planted predominantly with lime-lovers, especially if the local stone is used as a hard landscaping material. If a client wants acid-loving rhododendrons, the straightforward solution is to grow them in containers (filled with an acidic, or ericaceous, compost) and keep them on a patio or deck.

Incidentally, you will read in certain plant dictionaries that certain plants *need* acid soil. That's exactly right – they will die in alkaline conditions. Others, such as skimmias and the evergreen magnolia (*Magnolia grandiflora*), *prefer* acid soil. These will not die in alkaline conditions, but may not look particularly happy, developing yellow leaves. Be cautious.

SOIL STRUCTURE

Garden soil consists of two distinct layers overlying the parent rock (or bedrock). The uppermost layer is the one you're principally interested in. This should be a 30cm layer of moist, crumbly, dark brown or black loam – a mixture of even proportions of clay, silt, sand and humus (decayed plant remains and other organic detritus). Fertile topsoil is teeming with microbial life, an ecosystem all of its own that's responsible for supplying all the nutrients that plants need for healthy growth – a sobering thought, when you consider that we're dependent on this shallow layer for all foodstuffs.

The layer beneath this, generally lighter in colour, is the subsoil, likely to be of varying depth. This contains no nutrients at all. Plants cannot grow in subsoil, and roots that penetrate into this layer are responsible mainly for anchoring the plant in the ground.

SOIL TEXTURE

This is far more important than pH, and will determine how well the soil drains. It has a huge impact on plant choice and plant growth. Nearly all plants like nice, open, free-draining soil with a good humus content. You can tell at a glance if there's a drainage problem – there'll be telltale greenish film (the beginnings of lichen) on the soil surface. This indicates that water is not passing freely through the soil but instead is settling on the surface, encouraging algae, lichens and mosses (which love damp conditions). Moss on a lawn is another hint that the ground does not drain freely. Sorting out the drainage will be a priority (see 'Improving the soil', on p. 40).

A simple way to assess soil texture (which always impresses clients, incidentally) is to bend down and pick up a handful. Try rubbing this through your fingers as when you rub fat through flour to make pastry. If it binds into nice damp crumbs leaving your hands clean, you have the ideal – a nice 'friable loam'. If it stains your hands (and if you can squeeze it into a sausage in your hand), it's clay. If it fails to clump but blows away in a cloud of dust, you have a free-draining, sandy soil.

Heavy soils have a high clay content and tend to be muddy. This is the type that sticks to the soles of your boots and dries in solid lumps. In winter, they are cold and wet. In hot, rainless periods in summer, they dry out, setting like concrete and often cracking (a tell-tale sign to look out for). Heavy soils are difficult to work, and their tendency to consolidate makes it easy to ruin the texture. They are slow to warm up in the spring and cool down quickly in the autumn. That may not seem important, but it shortens the growing season by around a week or more at either end. Most importantly of all, they tend to freeze in winter (because of the water content). In a typical British winter, mild spells and cold snaps alternate – and it's this repeated wetting and freezing around the roots that kills many plants, not low temperatures themselves.

It's not all bad news, however. Many plants thrive in heavy soils – the high moisture content retains important nutrients for plant growth, making them available over a long period. Growth is often correspondingly lush. Plants that thrive in this type of soil (sometimes characterized as 'soil that does not dry out') are often vigorous and quick-growing – sometimes to the point of being invasive – meaning it's easy to cover the ground in a short period.

The exact opposite applies to dry, sandy soils, on every count. Light and easy to work, they heat up rapidly and stay warm for longer. The downsides are that water drains away rapidly, so they are prone to dry out, and nutrients dissolved in the water are lost to the plants. There is an ongoing risk of losing the uppermost layer of valuable topsoil through erosion (especially on sloping ground and exposed sites), as strong winds strip off soil particles from the surface.

Again, it's not all bad news. Plenty of plants – many scrubby and of Mediterranean origin – are adapted to grow in poor conditions. Most of the woody herbs – lavender, sage, artemisia and rosemary – will thrive in light soils (equally, they often die off in clay soils, killed by excess wet in winter).

WATERLOGGED SOIL

This is a designer's nightmare – a soil that squelches underfoot, suggesting a high water table. Any footprints rapidly fill with water. You can test the drainage by digging a hole about 45cm deep, filling it with water, then leaving it for an hour or so. If, on your return, the water has not completely drained, leave it overnight. If all of it hasn't drained away after this time, there is a problem.

Jackie Herald

Bare patches on the lawn are caused by shade cast by the tree and foot traffic. Compaction will have compromised the drainage.

A wet site *can* be drained, but it calls for excavating the whole site (including removal of any turf) and installing a land drain in a herringbone formation that feeds into a ditch or soakaway to collect the water. Even where this is possible, I am cautious about land drains. They tend to drain the ground unevenly and silt up – meaning the job has to be done again. It's generally easier to consolidate the ground by judicious use of plant material – plants that naturally grow in bogs or soil that never dries out fully.

If the waterlogging is localized (i.e. in just a small patch of ground), it's more likely that there is a pan in the subsoil – a layer of rock or solid piece of clay. Dig down and break it up with an auger, pickaxe or just a spade, as appropriate.

BARE SOIL

A large expanse of bare soil should set the alarm bells ringing – it suggests a fertility problem. Normally, bare patches of ground are rapidly colonized by weeds. If the garden attaches to a new-build, there's a possibility that an unscrupulous builder has stripped off the topsoil and sold it on (it sounds cynical, but it does happen). Dig down and you may find that what soil there is has been used as a repository for all manner of rubble and other detritus, which will have to be dug out and skipped before you import fresh topsoil.

There's also a possibility (though this is less likely) that the soil has been poisoned to eradicate weeds. (This is one scenario where a soil test sent to a lab might be a good way forward.) Other than replacing the topsoil, you have little option but to wait for the product to leach through the ground until it is no longer active.

There's one instance where I would definitely consider digging up and replacing the topsoil – and this is if you have to replant an area that's been under a weed-suppressing membrane. I am no great fan of these, as they interfere with the natural exchange of gases that goes on between the air and the soil. Underneath a membrane – which is usually weighted down with gravel or bark chippings – soil particles tend to clog. Not only is the texture ruined, but the very medium itself is apt to become sour. Earthworms and other beneficial soil life just cannot thrive in these conditions. You'll generally find that if the plants have been in for several years, in all probability they will not be doing well.

Improving the soil

The texture of soils can be improved, and very rapidly, and this need not be expensive. Adding bulky organic material helps bind light soils into larger, more moisture-retentive crumbs. Equally, it makes heavy clay more open and fibrous, greatly enhancing drainage.

It's rarely necessary to replace topsoil, but if you do need to, it's usually sold by the cubic metre and delivered to the site. Get it from a reliable source. Some property developers, the unscrupulous ones referred to above, have been known to sell topsoil (taken from another property) but mixed with some of the subsoil, so the fertility may have been compromised.

SOIL IMPROVERS

You can buy soil improvers ready formulated from garden centres, bagged up like potting compost. These are usually based on animal manures, but should be sterile and weed-free. They are expensive to use in quantity.

ANIMAL MANURES

Farmyard manure (FYM) is widely available, especially in rural areas (sometimes cost-free). All animal manure must be well-rotted before you apply it or it will actually use up nutrients in the soil as it continues to decompose. Well-rotted FYM is odour-free. You can never gauge the nutrient quotient, and it may well not be particularly high – much will have come from animals that have grazed on grass alone. But these materials, especially horse manure, are excellent for adding bulk to light soils in particular. Depending on what the animals have been eating, they may contain weed seeds.

Bird manure (from chickens or pigeons) should be used with caution. Containing uric acid, its effect is positively caustic if it comes into direct contact with plant material. Unless you know it's well rotted (which is unlikely), use it as an activator in compost or the manure heap to speed up the process of decay.

You can either dig these materials in or simply spread them on the soil and allow the weather and earthworms to do the job for you. This is easiest if you are starting work on the garden in autumn/winter with a view to planting up the following spring.

MUSHROOM COMPOST

Spent mushroom compost (used for the commercial growing of mushrooms) is sometimes available. It is an excellent material, usually weed-free, but almost always with an alkaline pH (owing to the presence of chalk in the mix). This generally isn't a problem, but the material should not be used around acid-loving plants.

GRIT

You can improve the draining of heavy soils immeasurably by forking in quantities of grit, either on its own or in conjunction with another soil improver. Check, however, that it is not limey in origin, which may impact on the soil pH level. Grit is heavy. Just a compost-sized bag can be very difficult to move. But it can be ordered in quantity, delivered to the site just like topsoil, and lifted in by crane.

Try to resist the temptation to substitute building sand to improve the drainage, especially if you have some leftover from a hard landscaping project. This sand is very fine grade and tends to clump – defeating the object.

Clearing the site

A site that's covered in weeds should be cleared before you begin.

For annual and perennial weeds, such as bindweed and dock, it's quickest and easiest to use a systemic contact weedkiller that is absorbed by the plants. Don't worry about the environment. Any product that falls on bare earth breaks down on contact with the soil and is rendered inert. Apply weedkillers during dull, still weather (so they don't blow onto neighbouring plants – or into neighbouring gardens) when the weeds are in full growth, in mid- to late spring if possible, or early autumn. Many gardeners think that treating them in early spring just as they start to emerge is the correct time, but it's best to delay. With the leaves fully extended and presenting a larger surface area, the product will be more effective. If you have to clear a site when the weeds are dormant and underground, use a pre-emergent weedkiller. Unlike a systemic weedkiller, this will persist in the soil for a while, so check the label before replanting the site.

Few modern weedkillers will deal with ground elder, which is particularly invasive and pernicious. The only reliable way of eradicating this is to remove and skip the affected soil, along with all the roots, and replace with fresh topsoil.

Woody weeds such as brambles and elder should be chopped down. The topgrowth may have to be skipped, but you may be lucky enough to be able to burn it on site. Treat the stumps with a brushwood killer to prevent regrowth or dig them out. If the brambles are relatively young,

A neglected space that's been used as a tip can be disheartenting – but you need to look beyond this and see the potential of the site.

allow them to re-shoot, then treat the topgrowth with a contact weedkiller. Felling a tree will require a tree surgeon, who will cut it so it falls tidily and safely. Dig out the stump with a stump grinder. All remaining traces of the roots should be removed – otherwise they may rot in the ground, effectively poisoning the soil as surely as any chemical.

Using membranes

Various membranes can be spread over the ground, the idea being that they suppress weed growth. They do – up to a point.

If the area is not to be planted, for instance if you are creating a gravelled area next to a driveway, use an impermeable membrane, such as a heavy-duty plastic or other synthetic. Most membranes, however, have small perforations or are woven so they are water and air permeable (to some extent). This means that they suppress weeds but allow for plants to be grown through them. Treat the area with a weedkiller first and carry out any soil improvement before spreading the membrane over.* Secure it in position at the edges either by digging a trench and burying

*Membranes are also commonly used under a deck, to suppress weeds. In this case, soil improvement is not necessary.

the edges or by weighing it down with bricks or stones. Cut crosses in the membrane for the plants, peel back the corners, plant, then fold back. You can disguise the membrane with a mulch (see below).

So far, so good. But I wonder about the long-term success of such plantings. Membranes, as mentioned above, tend to ruin the texture of soils and certainly have a negative impact on invertebrate life. Besides, how are you supposed to feed the plants? Sometimes their use is justified, in a front garden, for instance, that is planted for low maintenance, perhaps with a few slow-growing conifers. But useful as they are, they are not environmentally friendly and render any future work on the soil impossible.

Mulches

If you are going to use a membrane (sometimes the best option), you will have to top it with some material to disguise it. Stone chippings are often used. Make sure these integrate with the rest of the hard landscaping (and with any stone or brick in the neighbourhood). Slate has become popular almost to the point of being a cliché – and much is imported from China. Again, use it only if it's appropriate to the site.

Neither of these is a renewable resource, of course. Bark chippings are more organic, looking good in a wooded area. If you are really serious about 'sustainable' gardening, you might consider using builders' rubble (in fact, any of the detritus you uncovered on site) as a covering for a membrane. But however permeable the membrane, water is bound to collect around the mulching material. Bark chips tend to rot and may develop fungal growths, so may need to be replaced periodically. Stone chippings turn green with a film of algae, which can be treated with an algae killer.

A membrane and mulch do not necessarily spell the end of weed control, alas. Stray bits of roots left behind under the membrane sometimes shoot through it, and weeds can also seed in gravel and bark. They are usually easily removed by hand (or with a spot weedkiller) or – in gravel – they can be burnt off with a flame gun.

Choosing plants

If there is any subject on which designers need guidance, it is this one.

Use the site itself, its location and any plants that have to be retained (as well as any neighbouring gardens that are clearly visible, so have to be absorbed into the design) as your starting point. If you need to plant for low maintenance – and this is common in a professional brief – it makes sense to choose plants that are adapted to the prevailing conditions. Not only will they thrive and be problem-free, but they will tend to integrate with one another. Further guidance is given in the following chapters.

Plants for specific conditions

PLANTS FOR ACID SOIL	COMMON NAME
Abies	Fir
Arbutus	Strawberry tree
Berberidopsis corallina	Coral plant
Camellia	Camellia
Cassiope	
Desfontainia spinosa	Spiny desfontainia
Erica	Heather
Eucryphia	
Fagus	Beech
Gaultheria	
Gentiana sino-ornata	Gentian
Kalmia	Calico bush
Magnolia (some)	Magnolia
Pieris	
Primula (some species)	
Rhododendron	
Stewartia	
Styrax japonicus	Japanese snowbell
Styrax officinalis	Storax tree
Trillium	
Uvularia	
Vaccinium	Blueberry
Zenobia	

PLANTS FOR ALKALINE SOIL	COMMON NAME
Acanthus spinosus	Bear's breeches
Acer negundo	Box elder
Acer platanoides	Norway maple
Achillea	Yarrow

PLANTS FOR ALKALINE SOIL	COMMON NAME
Alyssum	
Aubrieta	
Aucuba japonica	Spotted laurel
Bergenia	Elephant's ears
Buxus	Box
Carpinus betulus	Hornbeam
Ceanothus impressus	California lilac
Cercis siliquastrum	Judas tree
Cistus	Rock rose
Clematis	
Cosmos	
Cotoneaster	
Dianthus	Carnation, pink
Eremurus	Foxtail lily
Forsythia	
Gypsophila paniculata	Baby's breath
Gypsophila repens	Creeping gypsophila
Hebe	
Helenium	
Helleborus	Hellebore
Juniperus	Juniper
Ligustrum	Privet
Lychnis chalcedonica	Jerusalem cross
Malus	Apple
Matthiola	Stock
Paeonia	Peony
Philadelphus	Mock orange
Pulsatilla	Pasque flower
Pyrus	Pear
Robinia	
Rosmarinus	Rosemary
Saxifraga	Saxifrage
Sedum	Stonecrop
Sempervivum	House leek
Sorbus aria	Whitebeam
Stachys	Bunnies' ears
Tagetes	African marigold, French marigold

Taxus baccata.	Yew
Tilia tomentosa	Lime
Verbascum.	Mullein
Viburnum	

PLANTS FOR LIGHT SANDY SOIL   COMMON NAME

Acanthus	Bear's breeches
Achillea	Yarrow
Anchusa.	Alkanet
Artemisia.	Wormwood
Ballota	
Clarkia	
Clianthus puniceus.	Parrot's bill
Coreopsis	
Cytisus	Broom
Dianthus.	Carnation, pink
Echinops ritro	Globe thistle
Erica	Heather
Eschscholzia.	California poppy
Gypsophila.	Baby's breath
Helichrysum	
Impatiens	Busy Lizzie
Lavandula.	Lavender
Limonium	Sea lavender
Nepeta x faassenii.	Catmint
Oenothera	Evening primrose
Passiflora.	Passionflower
Phlomis	
Rudbeckia hirta	Coneflower
Sedum.	Stonecrop
Sempervivum.	House leek
Tamarix	Tamarisk
Tropaeolum majus	Nasturtium
Yucca	

PLANTS FOR HEAVY CLAY SOIL	COMMON NAME
Amelanchier	
Aristolochia	Dutchman's pipe
Aruncus dioicus	Goatsbeard
Aucuba japonica	Spotted laurel
Caltha	Kingcup
Campsis	
Chaenomeles	Ornamental quince
Clematis	
Cornus alba	Dogwood
Cotoneaster	
Euonymus fortunei	Winter creeper
Forsythia	
Garrya	
Gunnera	
Hedera	Ivy
Kalmia	Calico bush
Lathyrus latifolius	Perennial pea
Lonicera	Honeysuckle
Lysichiton	American skunk cabbage
Mahonia	
Mimulus guttatus	Yellow monkey flower
Passiflora	Passionflower
Philadelphus	Mock orange
Primula (some)	
Pyracantha	Firethorn
Rheum	Ornamental rhubarb
Rodgersia	
Taxus	Yew
Trollius	Globe flower
Viburnum	
Wisteria	

PLANTS FOR WINDY EXPOSED SITES   COMMON NAME
(including coastal)

Alnus glutinosa	Common alder
Crataegus	Hawthorn
Elaeagnus x ebbingei	Elaeagnus
Euonymus japonicus	Japanese spindle tree
Hippophae rhamnoides	Sea buckthorn
Olearia macrodonta	New Zealand holly
Populus alba	White poplar
Quercus alba	American white oak
Rosa rugosa	Ramanus rose
Tamarix tetandra	Tamarisk

PLANTS FOR HOT DRY SITES   COMMON NAME

Artemisia	Wormwood
Cistus	Rock rose
Euphorbia characias	Mediterranean spurge
Euphorbia myrsinites	Broad-leaved glaucous
Lavandula	Lavender
Rosmarinus	Rosemary
Salvia officinalis	Sage
Stachys lanata	Bunnies' ears

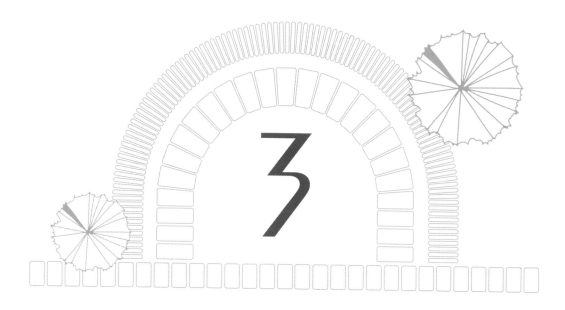

BALANCE, UNITY AND PROPORTION

When I first began teaching garden design, I was rather wary of this topic – because it is theoretical, dealing with ideas and abstractions. In fact, it has become the one I most look forward to – because of the excitement it engenders. Most people appreciate good design when they see it, but often feel they do not have the wherewithal themselves to create it. The aim here is not only to reveal design principles, but to persuade you to start thinking in design terms – and of yourself as a designer.

Some people are natural designers, occasionally without even being aware of it. They instinctively know how to arrange things so they look pleasing; they understand what works and what doesn't. There's no need to despair if you are not one of these lucky (possibly unlucky) people, as neither am I. The principles of design are easily assimilated and easy to apply – so long as you look beyond the theories to their possible practical applications. Some are suggested in the following pages, but others will spring to mind as you start thinking about your own garden (or other people's).

It's worth establishing at the outset why it's of value to know about design theories anyway. The fact is that when confronted by a bare plot of ground (and, soon, a blank sheet of paper) you have to make some design decisions very quickly – how wide to make the paths, how big to make the beds and borders, what the height of the pergola should be etc. Some knowledge of design principles can suggest possibilities, even if, as you develop the design, you find your-self overriding them (you will inevitably tweak them once you are on site). If nothing else, this knowledge can help you make a start, unlocking your creativity. Assume for one moment that you are a property developer who is renovating a house as a 'blank canvas', the aim being to create a neutral but pleasing space that a prospective buyer can easily make their own. While I hate the term 'kerb appeal', it's possible to make simple improvements to the exterior that will have a much more subtle impact than pots of winter pansies in clashing colours by the side of the front door. If, for instance, the garden – entirely reasonably – is to involve nothing more than new fencing, a patio and a lawn, giving some attention to the proportions can make all the difference between a property that looks as though you did the bare minimum and one that appears stylish and harmonious.

Now imagine that you have just stepped into someone's house for the first time. Entering the sitting room, you feel immediately welcome, at home. The furniture may not be of high quality, may not even match – but you are aware of a consistency in the way individual pieces are disposed around the room, the way they work with one another. To use designer-speak for a moment, it is a matter of 'volumes and voids' that involves not only the objects themselves, and their relationship to one another, but the spaces between them and the way they – as individuals and collectively – relate to the room's dimensions. Conversely, other homes are luxuriously furnished, maybe even with expensive designer or bespoke pieces, but somehow fail to add up. Natural designers have a flair for arranging the furniture – but even if you don't, applying some of the principles below can yield the same results.

You can carry an interior design analogy only so far, however, useful as it is. There are a couple of instances where trying to make any comparison between interior design and garden design breaks down. Emphatically, a room always has a ceiling, which a garden does not. That in itself defines proportions, whereas in a garden you can nearly always cast your gaze to the zenith, an immeasurable distance. Heights of walls, fences and hedges have an impact, of course, but they're not the same limiting factors as are the walls of a room, which are enclosed from above (some-thing you may find you can actually exploit when you come to make the garden). Second, pieces of furniture have fixed dimensions. In a garden, while certain elements stay the same, you also have to deal with plants that get bigger over the years, change shape or, in the case of bulbs, annuals and some perennials, disappear altogether for months at a time. Some trees and shrubs, solid masses for half the year, suddenly become skeletal in winter. Even if the hard landscaping persists, plants have a habit of flopping over onto paths, seeding themselves between paving stones and generally altering the scene from one season to the next.

One important point of contact, though, is that, when dealing with interiors, we nearly always place a premium on practicalities. That coffee table might be cunningly placed to line up with the window, but if it's too far from the sofa, you'll never use it to put your coffee on. Similarly, functionality remains important in a garden. The dustbins need to be given a space near the back door, paths need to be wide enough to move a lawnmower and wheelbarrow

Marshalls UK

The paved terrace uses proportions found in the adjacent house.

around, flower beds have to be deep enough to accommodate the plants. Be prepared to ditch the principles sometimes.

To strike an additional warning gong at the outset: a garden involves plants, which have to be allowed to grow. It may well be that some aspects of the design are not achieved straight away because they depend on the plants reaching maturity – which may not be for another five or even ten years after planting. This often has to be explained carefully to clients – they can express dissatisfaction when they notice you planting spindly trees. They have almost certainly envisaged fully grown ones, having effectively bought a garden on the basis of a finished drawing. Tact, diplomacy and gentle persuasion may be required.

Questions of style

Before going any further, there's an important distinction to be made between design and style. Design principles are universal – you find examples of good design everywhere, from Chinese temple gardens to Renaissance paintings, to contemporary art installations, and also in print media, especially advertising, which has to make an immediate impact (more on this next). These principles are easy to analyze and can readily be learnt.

Style, on the other hand, is personal, individual (as in 'that woman has style'); it is what makes you *you*. Actually, we all have style – a particular way of expressing ourselves, whether it's in writing, the way we dress, or simply how we move and speak – in all the things that give us identity. Unlike design, style is not quantifiable – you can't place a value on it. It can't be taught – in fact, it shouldn't be. If that seems like a blow – well, you will find your own style as a garden designer easily enough (and there are some hints in Chapter 10). Even though each garden I work on is different, I find myself doing the same things (or working in the same way) in each.

Unity

It's easiest to deal with unity first. In fact, unity is remarkably easy to achieve, even if you have been invited to work on an existing garden that seems to have been created haphazardly and in which (usually for financial reasons) a number of disparate elements have now to be retained. But what is unity?

In essence, it is that sense that the garden 'adds up', is all of a piece (assuming, for the moment, that this is desirable). If, as is usual, the garden can be seen from the house (and vice versa), it's nice – I don't want to put it any more strongly – if there's some palpable relationship between the two. While house and garden are distinct and separate, there should be some sense of belonging. As mentioned earlier, Gertrude Jekyll put it rather picturesquely: the garden should curtsey to the house. This is an interesting idea in itself. It gives the house a higher rank, with the garden being somehow 'subordinate' to the house. There is an implied dialogue between the two, with the house as the dominant speaker – the garden takes its ideas from the house, not the other way round. I'll suggest ways of putting this into practice further on.

Unity can be achieved with repetition of a particular colour, specifically with flicks – and I mean flicks – of red, something of a painter's ploy, or an interior designer's. You can achieve this with flowers if you are following the paintbox approach as used by certain gardeners (see Chapter 1) – but bear in mind that these are fleeting (more of the pitfalls are discussed in Chapter 5). A more permanent solution is to place matching containers or other objects strategically throughout the garden that provide a link from one area to another. Finalize their positions on site, when you can see how the whole scheme is coming together.

Another option is repetition throughout the site of particular eye-catching plants – the sort that don't integrate with their companions and need space around them. These are the ones that are sometimes referred to as 'architectural' (a term I loathe, at least when applied to plants) or 'accent' plants, which have a very specific value in this context (also, if used individually as focal points, of which more later). If there's space, Italian cypresses are unsurpassed and will give the garden the air of a Tuscan palazzo (be warned about that – it may not be appropriate). Otherwise, Irish junipers, which are much smaller, can be more biddable in northerly climes. In a very small garden, you might substitute upright rosemaries trained as pillars. Dome-shaped plants can achieve the same result, possibly more subtly. You might use box, clipped to shape, or the natural domes made by choisyas or some of the hebes. Note that these do not all have to be the same size – it is the repetition of the shape that supplies the sense of unity.

Spiky plants can work (I stress *can*) – by which I mean phormiums, yuccas and agaves (agaves are not hardy). A singleton in an impressive container can be a striking thing that can easily dominate a small garden (possibly desirable if you actually want it to be the stand-out feature). To limit the dominance, try placing two smaller specimens elsewhere – perhaps on a patio, possibly even as members of groups of other container plants. You may not immediately be aware of how it's done, but the garden will integrate, magically.

If you are going to use containers in a scheme with the intention of creating unity, please make sure they all match, though they don't have to be of the same size. Or that if one (or more) of them doesn't match, or even if they are all different, that it's for a reason. Assume for instance that you are going to incorporate a series of eight planters in your design. You may opt, perhaps on economic grounds, for traditional terracotta or even plastic. If you substitute for one of these a square container of the same material, or even just paint it a different colour, you introduce a certain quirkiness. It will stand out, even if they are all planted with the same plants.

You can also easily achieve unity by repetition of hard landscaping materials. As a general rule, as far as possible, I'd limit the range of materials to three at most. This is where it's possible to make a direct link between the garden and the house – if, for instance, there is a requirement for brick-built raised beds. Ideally, use the same brick as that used for the house, or as close a match as possible. If it's an old brick house, you may be able to source bricks of a similar vintage in a reclamation yard. If that's impractical, you can compromise by rendering the new brick, then painting it a more sympathetic colour to achieve the desired blend.

When deciding on the hard landscaping, much depends on choosing appropriate materials – appropriate to the house and its surroundings. If there are plenty of established trees around, by all means use decking – it will look completely natural. Decking is also suitable for a seaside garden – indeed, any garden that's by water where you would legitimately expect to find piers and decks. In a rural garden, use local stone if you can get it (and even if the house is not stone-built). In a city garden, where there's no requirement to make reference to adjoining countryside, anything goes. But don't be a slave to fashion. There's been a trend, recently, for using crushed Welsh slate both to cover a path – it snaps satisfyingly under foot – and as a mulch. This works well enough – in Wales, and other areas where slate occurs naturally, and maybe also in city gardens. But I have seen it used in gardens adjoining honey-coloured ironstone houses, which makes me wonder what the designer was thinking of. Equally, I've seen it used in a similar context but much more successfully – however, there it was a deliberate design choice, calculated to spring a surprise. Just be aware that all the choices you make have implications.

Of course, you're often not the one making the choices. You may find, for instance, that you are required to make a deck in a part of the garden that's visible from a paved terrace that has to

Repetition – of stoneware, colour and planting within a deliberately restricted range – makes for a restful, tranquil scheme.

remain – and the path linking the two has to be created with some third material. Here it may be a matter of running a line of bricks around all of them to unite them with one another and with the house – or by simply placing a large container on the terrace and a similar one on the deck beyond. You may find yourself working on a garden that already contains several disparate elements that have to remain (usually on the grounds of economy). In this instance, you are looking at damage limitation. Concealment can be a good option (see also the discussion on focal points and concealment). You may be able to screen out the offending object, maybe with a fence panel, hedge or a planting scheme that effectively blocks it out. Then you will have the added drama of the reveal – whereby something unexpected comes into view.

You can also achieve unity in a garden through a calculated use of proportion – but more on this later.

Balance

Before looking at balance closely, a word on symmetry – which is related. Symmetry is easy to define. Something that is symmetrical can be divided down the middle to produce two equal parts, one the mirror image of the other.

Symmetry is always pleasing, and is found not only in a vast number of household objects but also throughout the natural world. All flowers are symmetrical, leaves are often arranged symmetrically on stems, and the human faces often described as beautiful are symmetrical to a high degree. In a garden, symmetry implies extreme formality, control and use of even numbers. Bearing in mind plants' habit of growing, symmetry is usually achieved through regularly clipping suitable subjects into shape. Historically, symmetry is characteristic of the Italian and Islamic traditions. It's probably significant that many grand houses (or those with that aspiration) are laid out symmetrically. Symmetry, apparently, equals wealth and status.

In practice, symmetry, so simple in concept, is extremely difficult to achieve – angles have to be absolutely accurate, as does the placing of all the elements that make up the scheme. If you

Marshalls UK

These symmetrical beds are also well-proportioned.

Peter Anderson

Designs using symmetry need absolute precision in their execution, but note that the yew hedges to the left and right are unequal.

don't already do it, try lining up the objects on your mantelpiece symmetrically, and see how long you spend fiddling with them till you get it right. It can be hardest of all in a small garden that's enclosed by a wall or fence, as you'll soon realize when you measure the site (how you do this is dealt with in Chapter 10). Although the garden may present as a perfect rectangle, it's unlikely that the angles are true and the lines absolutely straight. If you are still determined to go down the symmetrical route – and it can be supremely effective – you will need to find a way of disguising the wayward angles, which is easiest with bold planting.

Interestingly, however, plants always retain a certain integrity. In an avenue of upright conifers (such as the planting of pencil junipers in the rose garden at Castle Howard), although their planting positions have to be strictly plotted, it matters little if, as they grow, they do not achieve exactly the same height or one or two billow out, or even lean out of line slightly. This tends to happen naturally as the plants mature, and is what gives life to a very strictly controlled scheme. Even tightly clipped box hedges tend to throw out the odd wayward stem or show a few bald patches here and there.

Whether or not you are following a strictly formal route, watch out for unintentional symmetry. If, for instance, you have adopted the strategy of repeating a plant throughout a design to achieve unity, you may find that from a particular standpoint two are clearly in your frame of vision. The eye constantly flicks between them. Placing a third element somewhere between the two – it might be another one of the same plant, a different one, or even a bird bath, obelisk, statue or container on a plinth – will resolve the issue. Pay attention to unintentional symmetry also when you're appraising a garden as part of your site survey (as detailed in Chapter 2). You'll need to find a way of resolving it.

Unlike symmetry, however, balance is more subjective, more a matter of perception. Whether

46

a design is symmetrical or not is cut and dried, but balance is in the eye of the beholder, as you are dealing with disparate elements. Fundamentally, it comes down to one's sense of mass or weight.

In the image above (Van Gogh's *Bedroom in Arles*), there is a clear division of the space left and right – with an implied vertical line that runs down through the left post of the bed's head-board. While one half is not a mirror image of the other, our sense is that the combined weight of the two chairs, table and window frame is equivalent to that of the bed. (Interestingly, the doors to either side of the painting underline the sense of balance.)

In the garden, balance can often be achieved by using similar volumes. Assume, for instance, that there is a bulky conifer in the garden that locks your attention. If, say, it's around 2m in height, you may be able to balance it with a 2m-long bench, placed nearby – something that occupies a similar amount of space (the fact that it is flipped over is entirely to the point here – you are not aiming at symmetry). Bearing in mind that the two should appear to be of similar weight, and that conifers are heavy plants, the bench should be made of solid teak or cast iron rather than lightweight aluminium.

This is an example at its simplest level – but when is life ever like that? What if the client *wants* aluminium garden furniture? In this scenario, your sense of the objects' weight comes

47

The imposing bamboo to the left is balanced by a shrubby hydrangea and seating.

In this scheme, the firm lines of the concrete walls would dominate unless they were balanced by the undulating planting and metal sculpture in the foreground.

The floating bench stops the eye from rushing headlong towards the planting seen through the opening – and also balances the steps to the left.

OASE (UK) Ltd

A clever use of proportion – not only between the house and the pool but within the water itself. The swimming pool and the irregular wildlife pond occupy a similar area.

into play. Without digging up the conifer and weighing it, you sense you would need a large group of aluminium furniture to balance it. In this case, it really does come down to your instinct, and is the kind of thing you may end up resolving only on site. You will probably need to move the furniture around to achieve a satisfactory effect. (This is one instance where it's quite possible to improve the design of an existing site without necessarily adding or taking anything away.) And if it's a small garden where there's only room for a bench to balance the conifer, consider placing a heavy stone or terracotta container next to it (possibly planted with another conifer) to 'weigh it down'. You can also achieve balance with plants – a pool-like planting of herbaceous perennials and grasses (perhaps even another, but smaller, conifer) could well help you offset an otherwise too-dominant feature.

It's impossible to predict all the problems you are likely to encounter, or suggest solutions, as each garden is different. Nevertheless, it's useful to be aware of some strategies that can help you solve design problems. This is one of those areas where your creativity comes into play, and the

Haddonstone

A pair of classically inspired stone troughs – in the 1:1 ratio – mark the start of a path.

best way to learn is by experiment – in your own garden, in your sitting room, or even with a few objects on your desk.

Proportion

Proportion, in design terms, means the relationship between different elements based on their size alone. You can use classic proportions that are found everywhere, or proportions that derive from the garden itself.

Possibly the most pleasing of all proportions is the obvious 1:1, the mirror image – which can be applied more often than you might think, even if you are not going down the route of exact symmetry. One of its most effective uses is immediately outside the house. Happy is the owner of the property whose front garden is the same length as the height of the house (and you can ignore the roof, which reads as a separate entity) – a real instance of a garden 'curtseying' to the house.

If you ever find yourself having to create a patio, terrace or deck to adjoin a bungalow, simply use the height of the bungalow to determine its depth. 'Makes a strong statement' is something I commonly read in the garden design context, as though inanimate objects and plants are capable of giving voice. However, I think it is true that the 1:1 ratio does 'make a statement' in so far as it always appears strong and not accidental, but without ever appearing contrived. In this respect, it is closely allied to symmetry and can give a suggestion of formality immediately outside the house.

THE GOLDEN RATIO

A classic proportion that is found everywhere is the golden ratio, sometimes also referred to as the golden section or golden mean. To achieve this, you divide a line in such a way that the relationship between the shorter of the two sections to the larger is the same as that between the larger section and the whole.

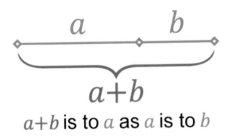

$a+b$ is to a as a is to b

If you can't get your head round this, relax. What you are really looking at above is the way the line $a + b$ has been divided. In practice, it comes out as a 'golden' ratio of 1:1.6 (and in the above, b is the 1 and a the 1.6); 1.6, incidentally, is necessarily an approximation. Like *pi*, it's an irrational number whose precise value cannot be calculated – the numbers after the decimal point extend infinitely (hence historically it's also been known as the divine ratio). But for our purposes, 1.6 is good enough.

Goya's *Third of May*. Note the use of the golden ratio.

Jackie Herald

The proportions of these arches are based on the golden section.

This proportion is always pleasing, and occurs throughout the natural world – in the spiral of a snail shell, for instance, and in the arrangement of seeds in a sunflower head. It's often found in works of art, and once you've learnt to recognize it you'll see it everywhere, especially in print advertising.

In the image to the left (Goya's *Third of May*), the composition can be split vertically into two balanced halves: left and right. But the implied horizontal rule that runs through the captive's hands and the soldier's hats divides the frame top/bottom into two areas that are in the golden ratio.

So how are you going to use the golden ratio in a garden? It can help you decide the depth of a border that runs along a wall, or fence, for instance, or – a textbook use – to determine the distance between the uprights of a pergola or covered walkway. The height of a pergola is usually determined by practical considerations, with just over 2m being the lowest (to allow adequate headroom once the pergola is covered in plants). Having settled on this, either divide or multiply the length of one upright by 1.6, then decide which of those values works best in the given situation.

FIBONACCI NUMBERS

Making the necessary calculations using 1:1.6 can result in some awkward values. It is sometimes simpler to use Fibonacci numbers instead, which will be familiar to anyone prepared to admit to having read Dan Brown's *Da Vinci Code*. The sequence runs:

0 1 1 2 3 5 8 13 21 34, etc.

with each number being the sum of the preceding two. (Fibonacci was the sobriquet of the early Renaissance Italian mathematician Leonardo Pisano Bogollo.) You have to start with 0 and 1 to get the sequence going.

The way to use Fibonacci numbers in a design context is to isolate two adjacent numbers. Ignoring the initial zero (which literally has no value), you immediately find our old friend 1:1. The ratio 1:2 – so I've been told – is often used by florists when deciding the height of the finished arrangement relative to the vase. I suggest that in the garden you go a bit further down the sequence. In fact, the further down the sequence you go, the closer you get to the golden section – 21 x 1.6, for instance, is 33.6, not so far off the 34 you get using Fibonacci. The 5:8 ratio is often the simplest. To come back to the border running along the fence scenario, for a shallow border measure the height of the fence, divide by 8, then multiply the answer by 5; for a deep one, divide by 5 then multiply by 8. In other words, if the fence is 2m high, a border of 1.25m would work well. If space allows, opt either for a 2m border (1:1) or – very grand – 3.2m (5:8).

Just how satisfying Fibonacci numbers are can be seen in the following diagrams:

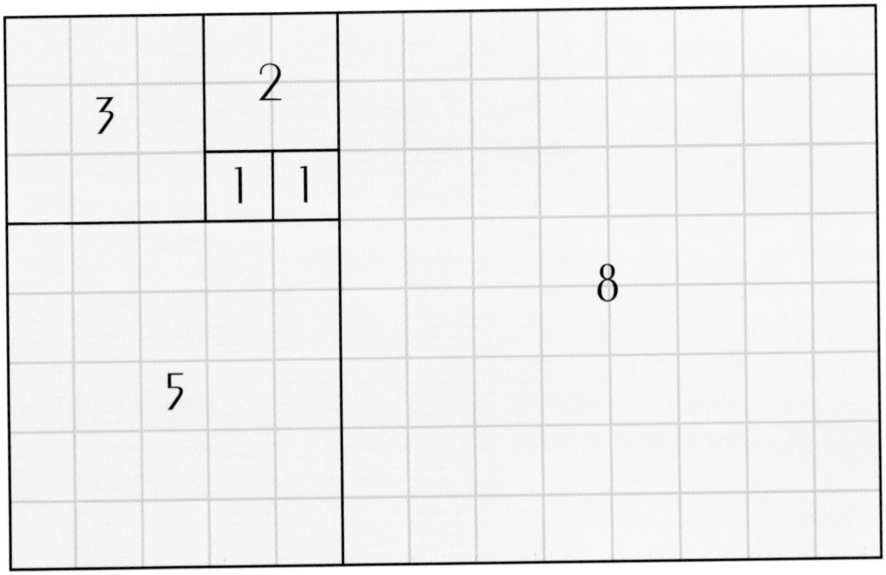

Nobody is saying that you *have* to lay out a garden this way – or, as in the previous illustration, conceive the design as involving a system of squares – but these proportions are always pleasing to the eye and can help you make decisions about the size of the lawn or deck or width of a path or border relative to some other aspect of the site.

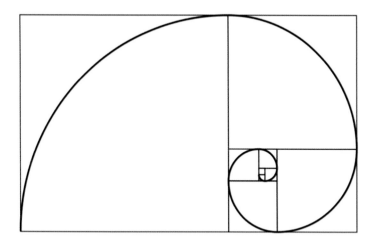

There's rather an (intentionally) literal application of this principle at Boughton House in Northamptonshire, in the garden developed by Kim Wilkie. That's a garden on the grandest scale, but the Fibonacci sequence can also be of inestimable value to the property developer referred to previously who just wants to lay out a basic garden with a lawn, a path and a few borders. Even if the garden is unplanted (apart from the lawn), you can make the most basic design appealing by using the Fibonacci sequence.

I can't stress too highly that all of this should be viewed as a means to an end – it's merely a strategy to help you start carving up space – and not an end in itself. There's a different card you can play on the proportion front – and this is to repeat in the garden some of the proportions observed in the house (and thus neatly realizing that Jekyllean curtsey – if that's the route you want to go down).

Stand in the garden and look back at the house. Your eye may well be drawn to the back door or sitting room window or some other feature. Choose whichever strikes you as most prominent, then measure it. These measurements provide you with proportions that you can repeat in your design, thus creating a subtle link between the garden and house. It's an effective way of creating unity if, for some reason, you have to use widely diverging materials – the unity will be in the proportions. Imagine, for one moment, that you have to create a second seating area in a garden where there is an existing paved patio that abuts the house. Economics – or the client – may dictate that the new seating area is a low-cost deck. The two materials may be completely disparate, but you can unite the two by basing the proportions of the new deck on the patio.

The link works even if you decide to place the deck on the diagonal – if anything, it would be more subtle.

Note that we are talking about proportions, not exactly repeated sizes. Say you choose a window on which to base some new elements in the garden and this measures 1.2m x 2.2m (incidentally: *always* use metric, it makes the maths so much easier). If you wish to decide the length of a raised bed that you know has to be 95cm wide, simply divide 95 by 1.2 then multiply by 2.2. You'll end up with a length of 174cm (I don't think it would matter much if you rounded this up to 175). Nor do you need to restrict yourself to rectangles. If you wish to dig an oval or kidney-shaped bed into a lawn, provided it fits into a rectangle of the same proportions you can achieve the same link. There'll be more on this in Chapter 10 with the discussion on grids.

Haddonstone

A classical urn marks a focal point at the end of a path. Note the proportion between the urn and the supporting plinth. Being white, it looms large in the scheme – at dusk it will appear closer than it is.

Focal points and concealment

A focal point is something that draws the eye and dominates. To all intents and purposes, a focal point (in a garden) is some striking object (be it a bird bath, fountain, statue, obelisk or large decorative container) or plant, such as a tree or large shrub that, without competition from near neighbours, has achieved its natural proportions. It might even be one of the 'architectural' plants referred to on p. 42. A focal point is not by any means essential in a garden, but it does provide a sense of purpose, creating a kind of dynamism, in so far as you feel ineluctably drawn towards it. You can use a focal point to mark the end of a path, or the meeting of two or more paths. Historically, focal points are characteristic of many very formal, not to say deliberately stylized, gardens (as explored in Chapter 1). But focal points can also play a part in a more informal design. Look round any established garden, and you may well find that there are already focal points within it, possibly unplanned, jumping out at you. If there are several striking features, the eye is confused, and the potential impact of any one of them is considerably diminished through the competition of the others.

You can plot a course around a garden by using a series of focal points but it should be planned so that only one of them is in view from any standpoint, with the others remaining hidden. As you arrive at one focal point, another comes into view, then from that one a third focal point. This principle was certainly used historically (as outlined in Chapter 1*), but can also be applied on a more domestic level. Assume a focal point draws your eye the minute you step outside the back door. When you reach it, you turn, and a second one, invisible from the back door, is revealed. Concealment of this from the house can be achieved by judicious use of fencing, hedges or perhaps just a thick planting – as, for instance, if the first focal point is a mature tree that dominates the garden. A seat placed near the trunk (a shady retreat in summer) and a path leading to it invite you to walk towards it. On sitting down you take note of a second focal point, in this case a fountain in a pool.

*For instance, at Sissinghurst, there is a view through the white garden to the statue of a Bacchante that marks the end of an avenue of pleached limes. On reaching the statue, if you turn ninety degrees to look along the avenue and through the nuttery beyond, your eye alights on a large shallow planter in the herb garden. As you progress along the avenue, a view through to the South Cottage is revealed.

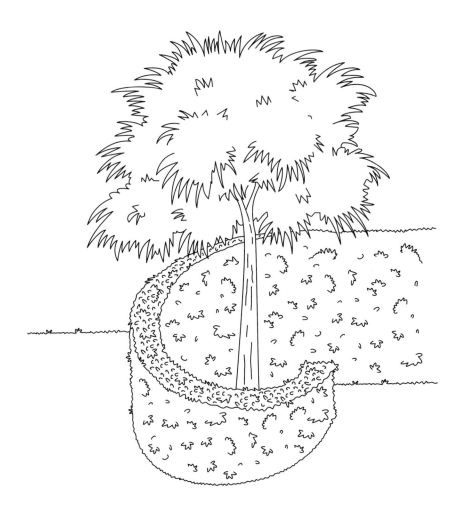

Concealment is worth considering if you are working on an existing garden that already contains a number of striking features that refuse to integrate – for instance, a tall conifer and a summerhouse some distance away in an otherwise open site. The attempt to create balance has defeated you. Consider instead the feasibility of concealing one of them with, as suggested, a hedge, fence or thick planting. You can also extend this principle in order to bring an element of surprise to a garden – by which I mean raising an expectation then thwarting it. Assume for a moment that you have a rectangular garden. You have planned the area outside the house very formally: a straight central path, flanked with regularly spaced upright conifers, leads through an archway cut into a strictly pruned hedge. From the house, you can see, through the archway, a fountain. On walking down the path and through the archway, you discover that the fountain is placed off centre in an irregularly shaped pool, which is itself part of a garden planted to attract wildlife. On this side, the hedge is clipped much less formally and is a backdrop to an apparently random scheme of rocks, wildflowers and unmown grass. From the house, the fountain – the focal point – reads as the culmination of the formal scheme, but turns out to be only a part of something else entirely. There is a brilliant example of just such a ploy at the Menagerie at Horton, created by Gervase Jackson-Stops. A straight grass path leads between tall hornbeam hedges towards a Gothic hut that acts as the focal point. The sense of confinement between the hedges is almost threatening (probably as a result of their excessive height relative to the width of the path). You walk through the hut to be confronted by an unexpectedly large lake – the sense of release is palpable.

False perspectives and foreshortening effects

You can create a greater sense of depth in a garden by using false perspective. The underlying principle is that objects appear smaller the further they are away from us. A classic method is to make a straight path narrow towards its destination. From the wider end of the path, it therefore appears longer (from the other end, the effect is reversed). If you line the path with clipped box balls or upright conifers, they should be progressively smaller as the path narrows if you wish to heighten the illusion. Historically, false perspective was much used in Italian Renaissance gardens, as described in Chapter 1.

Exploiting the same principle, there are other visual tricks you can play. If, for instance, you place a container prominently near the back door, then a similar one – but of different size – some distance away, you can either lengthen or shorten the perspective. The viewer is fooled into thinking that the two containers must be of the same size. If the one in the garden is the smaller, it will appear to be further away than it actually is; if larger, then closer. If it's the smaller one that's in the garden, raising it on a plinth confuses the eye further.

So what's the point of this? While moving from a large object to a smaller one might make the garden seem longer than it is (particularly if you also lay out the path that leads to it with a false perspective), why bother making it seem smaller? Well, it produces a pleasingly dramatic effect. The large object will appear to be close at the outset, but then apparently move away from you as you advance towards it.

Something similar happens – or can be made to happen – if the garden has a slope. This can be particularly apparent if the slope is a steep one. The effect is dependent on the extent to which we are able to judge distances. This was brought home to me recently when I was asked to give advice on a garden that presented a very particular problem. Here the garden begins on a much lower level than the house – at the back of which is a deck that incorporates steps leading down to the garden proper. The land then continues to fall away to the boundary. To the right, and filling the garden on that side, is a stand of mature trees that have a preservation order on them. This creates a site of unexpected drama, not yet fully exploited.

The way this 'drama' plays out is as follows. Standing on the deck and looking straight ahead rather than down at the ground – the trees invite this – the trees appear to 'stack up', seeming to be closer together than they actually are when you are physically among them. The distance between the trunks as you look at them in the horizontal plane is rather less than the distance between each tree at ground level, where the slope of the ground puts a greater gap between each. Hence, viewed from the deck the garden appears smaller than it actually is. It is only when you are in it that you get a true sense of its size. Walking down the garden, the trees then apparently retreat. Added to this, at the bottom of the garden, beyond the last of the trees, is a second deck with table and chairs. From the house, this 'reads' as being very small – a small object viewed close. Only *en route* do you appreciate its actual dimensions.

Reversing this, gardens sometimes contain quite steep banks rising from ground-floor level. As mentioned in Chapter 2, these sites lend themselves to rockeries, cascades and watercourses. If you are using rocks, placing larger ones at the top and smaller ones towards the bottom will make the slope appear steeper, rearing up in front of you. (If they were all the same size, the ones at the top would appear smaller because they are further away.) Do the reverse and the slope will appear gentler. The true topography is only revealed when you climb up it.

As you grasp and begin to think of possible applications of these ideas, you will soon find yourself thinking in terms of 'manipulating the space' – rather like André Le Notre at Versailles. At that point, it might be worth taking a step back. While there are any number of 'tricks' you can play, I'd urge caution – they can make a garden seem contrived. My own view is that a design should appear inevitable – the most elegant solution to a given problem. So I stress that what have been discussed here are principles, not rules – there is no prescription that leads to successful design. You'll learn by doing, not studying.

CHOOSING PLANTS FOR THE GARDEN: TREES, SHRUBS, CONIFERS AND CLIMBERS

A garden has to contain plants – indeed, for many people, plants are the be-all and end-all of gardening. This chapter deals with the woody plants, the plants with a permanent above-ground framework that are a presence year-round. This is something that's often overlooked and applies to deciduous plants – the ones that shed their leaves in autumn – as much as evergreens. Their bare skeletons can be a strong feature during the dead of winter. Never underestimate the impact their shadows will make on a clear winter's day. Their height has a huge influence on the proportions of the garden – they lift the eye away from the boundaries.

These plants are sometimes referred to as the 'backbone' of the garden – not a bad analogy, if you think of a garden as a living thing. But always when using these plants, it's good to have an idea of how you want things to look in the longer term. These plants will probably be around for a long time and down the years will also change shape. Like people, some gain character as they age while others spend their energies rapidly before experiencing a raddled middle age.

I am cheating slightly by including the climbers here. They are indeed mainly woody, but a few die back completely, disappearing below ground (and some that don't, such as the clematis, can hardly be called major players when they are out of leaf). But as most are such big-scale plants with a long life, it's worth dealing with them here.

There is a definite hurdle to be crossed here when you're at the planning and planting stage. Full-size mature trees and shrubs are expensive and often not worth the candle, as they can prove difficult – and therefore costly – to manoeuvre and need regular watering during the first year to help them establish. In fact, they may not establish at all. For reasons of both cost and practicality, you are far more likely to be planting trees that are still at the sapling stage and small shrubs. This need not concern you if you are dealing with your own garden and can easily see the bigger picture, as it were, but it can present an issue for professionals. As mentioned earlier, clients often feel – and express – disappointment when they see the small and spindly specimens you have planted. It just has to be explained to them that trees and shrubs will need time to establish and then take a few years before they achieve the beautifully balanced scheme you have devised.

Several trees and shrubs (including conifers) have a utility value as material for hedging. There's more on this in Chapter 8.

Some definitions

Botanically, there's no difference between trees and shrubs – both are plants with woody stems. The difference is one of scale and, to a lesser extent, habit. Most of us would understand a tree as being about 5m tall, probably more in time, and with a single trunk and a spreading or rounded crown of upper branches. Trees have a tendency to grow straight upwards, competing with one another for light, developing slim trunks as they go. Shrubs tend to top at the 3m mark and are usually multi-stemmed. Having said that, certain trees, such as the birches (*Betula*) and eucalyptus, can develop two or more trunks from the base, and shrubs such as rhododendrons can become tree-like with age, with a strong leader, or trunk, and spreading crown. In the wild, shrubs often, but not always, form the understorey among stands of trees or appear at the margins of forested areas (there's a clue there in how to use them sympathetically in a garden). They have a tendency to be rangy as they stretch upwards towards the light filtered by the leafy tree canopy above them.

In a very tiny garden, there may be no room for a tree, in which case a large shrub can fulfil a similar function. But there's no way that a tree – or large shrub – should be considered essential in any design. In a windswept or coastal garden, or one with a spectacular view, you may well decide to dispense with taller plants altogether.

Specimens

This is not what you deliver to the health centre – in the garden, a specimen is understood as a plant seen in splendid isolation; in other words, with space around it so it can achieve its natural habit to be viewed from all sides. This is in distinction to the mixed planting, where the lower portions of a tree (or shrub) might be hidden by other lower-growing plants, or the shrubbery, in which shrubs are massed together and merge cosily like kittens in a basket. In a small garden, a specimen will have undoubted presence, and should therefore be chosen with care. Not only will it have – usually – an annual period of unmatched splendour and be a real eyecatcher, but it should be good enough not to be an eyesore at other times.

No one is saying you have to have a specimen tree or shrub in a garden. But if you want a dominant feature from which the rest of the design will appear to radiate out, a large tree or shrub will do the job for you. And a large tree, to some extent, puts a 'ceiling' on the garden. It lifts your eye, but not to the zenith, and can help define the space overall. The canopy of a mature tree creates a 'volume' above eye level.

In design terms, a specimen is excellent for creating a focal point.

TREES

Above all, trees, being generally long-lived plants, give a garden a sense of permanence. In time, they confer an air of maturity, provide shelter and a nesting place for birds, lift the eye skywards and cast (often welcome) shade in summer. They can also screen or distract from an ugly view. Trees are often selected for some particular ornamental feature – but bear in mind that this may be of short duration or may take some time to develop. Also that 'year-round interest' (of which more anon) can often equate to 'year-round dullness'. Don't forget also that trees grow and change shape. Some remain almost symmetrical during the first decade after planting, but lose their firm outline with the years – they can, however, like people, gain other qualities. Shrubs can often be pruned to rejuvenate them, but the same does not apply to trees (or very rarely).

PRACTICAL CONSIDERATIONS

If you take the reasonable view – as I suggest you do – that you should choose plants that will thrive in the given situation (see Chapter 2), you will find your choice usefully restricted. The limitations of a site are as important a consideration as the possibilities and this is particularly true of any plant that you intend for the longer term. A tree planted in unsuitable conditions will fail to thrive – indeed may not grow at all – and will be subject to a whole raft of pests and diseases. The best advice is to visit a local tree nursery and outline your needs to the owner. It's not in their interest to sell you plants that will fail.

The number one consideration must be the hardiness of the plant (and bear in mind that young trees, especially conifers, are more vulnerable to cold than established ones, and may need some protection in the initial stages). If you are choosing an early-flowering tree, make sure it doesn't flower at a time when you anticipate frost – which could ruin the flowers. Obviously you cannot predict the weather year by year, and it's almost inevitable that magnolia flowers, for instance, will be ruined at some point – they are often produced at times of the year when hard frosts are common. But it would be madness to plant one in a known frost pocket or on an east-facing wall – opening flowers touched by an air frost overnight can scorch when the rising sun hits them.

Soil type is also important. Many trees won't tolerate waterlogged soil, others will thrive in it – and in fact can do a good job of consolidating wet ground. Check the rate of growth – young trees can take a couple of seasons to settle, then suddenly shoot off (which may need explaining to clients, who may worry about apparent slow progress). Contingent on that is the ultimate size of the tree and how long it will take to achieve it. An often neglected consideration is the impact that the tree will have on the rest of the garden – not only will it become a dominating feature in time, stealing attention from other features, but it will suck up moisture from the ground (to the possible detriment of grass and any other plants in the vicinity), maybe not in the short term, but almost certainly in the years to come. Think also of the shade the mature tree is likely to cast during the summer and make this a positive aspect of the design (perhaps by planning for a shady deck or terrace to be a retreat during hot weather). Be especially cautious about planting trees near boundaries with neighbouring gardens. The people next door might enjoy a flowering cherry as much as your clients in spring, but then seethe with resentment when it casts a dark shadow over their patio in summer while you are basking in sunshine.

Put in those terms, a tree's obvious decorative features will often end up fairly well down the list of criteria.

ORNAMENTAL FEATURES

Even though a tree will be a permanent fixture in the design, most have a period of the year when they are of particular interest – because of their flowers, fruits, young foliage, autumn foliage or bark.

There is a plethora of spring-flowering trees. My own feeling is that Japanese cherries (*Prunus*), beautiful as they are and of which there are a vast number from which to choose, belong in Japan – where they are planted in great avenues and provide a romantic setting for young couples to declare undying love to one another. My objection to them is that they make such big trees, generally more spreading than they are tall – and their moment of glory is comparatively brief (a mere two weeks in spring). If you have room, fine – but be aware that when in full leaf in summer they have a distinctly leaden look, casting dense shade. Pruning cannot rectify this – it quite ruins their natural shape. If you must have a cherry, the only one that remains really recommendable, for a small garden at least, is 'Amonagawa', with several stems rising upright from the base to a height of 3–4m – more of an upright shrub, really.

As an alternative, the crab apples (*Malus*) are generally smaller, with a more rustic, homely, less sophisticated manner. If you want to go really rustic, try a hawthorn (*Crataegus*), if you can stand the fishy smell of its May-time flowers. Also delightful are amelanchiers, ideal in a small garden, and the ornamental pears (*Pyrus calleryana* and *Pyrus salicifolia* 'Pendula'). Sorbus are also excellent, somewhat larger but usually with an open airy canopy that casts little shade in summer – often an important consideration. Magnolias are slow-growing but magnificent when mature, with a spread that's comparable to their height. Unlike many other deciduous trees, they are worth looking at even when out of leaf, with gracefully spreading branches like a candelabra.

Branching from low down on the trunk, they often have the appearance of large shrubs.

Japanese maples (forms of *Acer japonicum* and *Acer palmatum*) are often extremely pretty as the new leaves – bright coral red, soft buff green or even shrimp pink – burst from the bare stems in late winter to early spring. Flowers are not needed. The plants are perfectly hardy, but to protect those delicate young leaves they need a site sheltered from strong winds, heavy rainfall (which can rip through the leaves) and direct sun. They are really more like large shrubs that in the wild would appear at the margins of forests, sheltered by a canopy of leaves above them.

For summer flowers, choice is more limited. On the cusp of spring and summer a laburnum, with its wisteria-like yellow flowers, can be quite a sight, but the seeds that follow them are poisonous, so this may not be the best option if you have small children. They flower at perhaps the last point in the year – late spring – when their rather hard yellow can be considered desirable.

Two alternatives are the Indian bean tree (*Catalpa bignoniodes*, also with yellow or purple leaves), with spires of orchid-like flowers in summer, and the foxglove tree (*Paulownia tomentosa*), with purple-blue, foxglove-like flowers. With their large, soft leaves, both need a sheltered position and flower best in the year following a hot summer (which ripens next year's flowering stems). They have other uses, however – see 'Special effects', on p. 68.

There is another invaluable tree, far too seldom seen: the Mount Etna broom – *Genista aetnensis*. This produces a shower of soft yellow pea flowers – like those of an ordinary broom – above head-height and is excellent for giving height to a 'Mediterranean' planting of woody herbs, cistus and other scrubby plants. Unlike the laburnum, the yellow isn't heavy because the plant itself is so light and airy.

For some reason, *Aralia elata* is not particularly popular, perhaps because of its suckering habit. Neither is *Sophora*, though this is not reliably hardy. *Eucryphias*, which flower in late summer, are seldom seen. Magnificent when studded with their white flowers, they are uncompromisingly tall and narrow – a difficult shape to work with – and most of them must have acid soil. And space.

AUTUMN INTEREST

Some trees are dual-purpose, in the sense that they provide further interest in autumn (possibly having been deadly dull all summer). A rare few have spectacular autumn leaf colour, though this can never be reliably predicted or planned for, and it's generally fleeting. Technically, the green chlorophyll in the leaves breaks down before the leaves are shed, briefly allowing other colours – red, orange and yellow – to become visible before autumn gales strip the leaves from the trees. But much depends on soil type, how warm the summer was and, indeed, what the prevailing autumn conditions are. It's difficult to plan (or plant) a garden for autumn leaf interest alone.

Some of the spring-flowering trees have excellent autumn fruits that can hang on the branches even after the leaves have fallen. Crab apple fruits are like baubles, red or bright golden yellow. Even more striking are the sorbus – some have bright red berries, but the species *Sorbus cashmiriana* and *Sorbus hupehensis* have pearl-like white berries that can show pink flushes. For all those who wish to attract wildlife into the garden, these are a valuable food source for birds. Ecologists might use these in combination with a wildflower meadow (see Chapter 6) and wildlife pond (see Chapter 7).

WINTER INTEREST

Winter-flowering trees are few and far between. The best – in so far as it's the hardiest – is the so-called winter cherry *Prunus subhirtella* 'Autumnalis'. The name is completely misleading. Yes, flowers appear in the autumn (though not in great quantity) and may even carry on opening spasmodically during winter – but in mild spells only. The real display does not start properly until late winter, or even early spring, segueing into the spring cherries discussed on p. 64. Like them, it is potentially a large tree. *Acacia dealbata* will flower in late winter, but needs a very sheltered spot in cold areas – and is also potentially large.

Often it's better to think outside the box. Many trees have good bark that suddenly becomes interesting when there's little else to look at. Several of the birches (varieties of *Betula utilis* with

Peter Anderson

Birches (*Betula*) are popular for their bark – here accentuated by the removal of the lower branches.

evocative names like 'Silver Shadow') have gleaming white bark, so the whole tree lights up the garden with its bare branches (particularly if planted where the winter sun will strike it). Even better, if you can find it, is *Betula albo-sinensis* var. *septentrionalis*, with creamy cinnamon pink bark (and butter yellow autumn leaf colour). If you have the space, *Prunus serrula* has gleaming rich brown bark (people have been known to take a duster to it to buff it up). Among the maples, *Acer capillipes* and *Acer davidii* (both referred to as snake-bark maples) have bark streaked with silver and white. On *Acer griseum* (paperbark maple) the bark peels off in patches, like wallpaper.

WHAT NOT TO PLANT

There are certain trees against which I have a particular, though well-founded, prejudice and would never consider planting:

Eucalyptus gunnii Frankly, this all-too-commonly planted tree belongs in its native Australia (in scrubland at that). So far from home, these eucalyptus never look right. Not without charm when young, they rapidly grow tall and gangly, their evergreen foliage becoming a dull pewter grey. If you must have a eucalyptus, keep it regularly pruned (see 'Coppicing and pollarding' on p. 68)* or – if there is room – consider the snow gum, *Eucalyptus pauciflora* subsp. *niphophila*, a (usually) multi-trunked tree with beautiful grey and cream flaking bark. Ultimately, they work best in city gardens where there is no need to make reference to the landscape outside the garden.

Rhus typhina the stag's-horn sumach. So-called because of its antler-like habit. Admittedly, the autumn leaf colour – a rich, glowing red – is sensational, but this is a rampant thing that spreads far and wide by means of underground suckers. I've seen it used to great effect on traffic islands, which is where it belongs. In a garden, it will soon be poking up through the lawn, in beds and borders, even through cracks in paving. (The form 'Laciniata', with lacy, finely dissected leaves, which is considerably less vigorous, is a much better option.) It is also quite likely to find its way into neighbouring gardens, potentially creating as much bad feeling as the shade-casting trees discussed previously.

Robinia pseudoacacia 'Frisia'. Widely encountered in suburbia, this is a tree 'valued' for its golden yellow foliage. A supposed advantage is that, unlike other yellow-leaved plants, it holds on to its colour throughout the summer. (Most yellow-leaved plants become progressively green.) That's a debatable distinction, but what tells against it, ultimately, are two definite disadvantages. Though often recommended for small gardens, it turns out to be extremely fast-growing and rapidly makes a very large tree. Second, the branches are extremely thorny and brittle – strong

*Mature specimens that have been allowed to get out of hand can be cut back to a 'hat-rack' of branches and generally recover well.

gales will rip them from the trunk, if not fell the whole thing. For a small yellow-leaved tree, *Gleditsia triacanthos* 'Sunburst' is a much daintier proposition – though by summer the bright yellow young leaves will have faded to plain green.

Special effects

While on the whole I think a tree should be allowed to be a tree – that is, to continue on its upward trajectory unimpeded – several lend themselves to certain pruning techniques that are not only decorative in themselves but keep the tree within manageable bounds. Some potentially large trees can thus be used in smaller gardens (though there is a certain amount of upkeep involved). Bear in mind, however, that there's generally a loss as well as a gain.

COPPICING AND POLLARDING

This involves the annual (or biennial) cutting back of all the previous year's stems to a low framework of stems (coppicing) or to a trunk perhaps 2–3m high (pollarding). These are traditional techniques used to produce quantities of whippy stems for use in fence-making and basket-weaving. Plants are cut back (annually or every two or three years) either for the appeal of the bare stems (which thus make a strong contribution in winter) or for larger leaves. There is always a loss – the plants will not flower or fruit and autumn leaf colour will not be so good.

Coppiced willows (*Salix*) and/or dogwoods (*Cornus*) make an ideal waterside planting, especially if they can be sited so the low winter sun lights up the stems and makes reflections in the water. (In the wild, they are often found growing by water, as they need damp soil.) Depending on the variety, stems are bright red, orange or yellow. A stand of coppiced *Rubus* (either *Rubus cockburnianus* or *Rubus thibetanus*) earn their name of ghost bramble when combined with early snowdrops and hellebores (emphatically *not* white crocuses – the white of these is too clear and unsubtle). If space permits, add a white-barked birch.

Catalpas and paulownias cut hard back each year produce larger-than-average leaves that give a lush, even tropical, look to the garden (while being fully hardy). Rigorously kept within bounds in this way, they can be included as foliage plants in large mixed plantings.

SHRUBS FOR COPPICING   COMMON NAME

Leaves

Berberis thunbergii	Japanese barberry
Corylus maxima 'Purpurea'	Filbert
Cotinus coggygria	Smoke bush
Sambucus racemosa 'Plumosa Aurea'	Red elder

Stems

Cornus alba.	Dogwood
Cornus stolonifera 'Flaviramea'	Yellow-barked dogwood
Rubus cockburnianus.	Ghost bramble
Rubus thibetanus.	Ghost bramble
Salix alba 'Britzensis'.	Scarlet willow
Salix irrorata.	Bluestem/sandbar willow

TREES FOR COPPICING OR POLLARDING   COMMON NAME

Leaves

Catalpa bignoniodes	Indian bean tree
Eucalyptus gunnii	Cider gum
Paulownia tomentosa.	Foxglove tree
Populus x jackii 'Aurora'.	Variated balm of Gilead
Robinia pseudoacacia.	Black locust
Toona sinensis 'Flamingo'	Chinese mahogany

Stems

Acer pensylvanicum 'Erythrocladum'	Moosewood
Salix acutifolia	Sharp-leaf willow
Salix alba	White willow
Salix daphnoides 'Aglaia'	Violet willow
Tilia platyphyllos 'Rubra'.	Red-twigged lime

Topiary

This is not a book on topiary, but simple shapes are easily achieved and topiary specimens, both large and small and ready-clipped, are available in bigger garden centres – and also from specialist suppliers. Plants usually used are the evergreens yew (*Taxus*), for large balls, obelisks, pyramids and columns, and box (*Buxus*) for smaller shapes. They are excellent for giving bulk and solidity to any scheme. Holly (*Ilex*), bay (*Laurus nobilis*) and privet (*Ligustrum*) are also sometimes used.

Standards comprise a ball of foliage on a clear length of stem. Top-heavy, these should only be used in a site sheltered from wind. Standards are often created artificially by grafting a small shrub onto a tall stem of a related plant. Evergreen euonymus are often treated this way, as well as a couple of flowering plants such as lilacs and roses.*

Certainly, if you are looking to achieve formality and symmetry, this is a good way to go, even in a small space – and such plants do give a space a gardenesque (in the true sense) air. You can even juggle around with perspective using plants of the same shape but in different sizes (or possibly using different plants – large and small obelisks of box and yew, for instance). Topiary specimens come into their own in winter, when their contribution to the design is strikingly apparent.

Topiary raises the stakes somewhat, as all such plants need regular clipping to keep them in shape. They cannot be called 'low-maintenance'. Topiary plants need trimming at least twice a year, in spring and mid-summer, and at other times as well if they are to maintain a firm outline. Even then, they will eventually outgrow the initial shape, and modifications may have to be made longer term.

TOPIARY WITHOUT TOPIARY

Some conifers make a naturally good shape with minimum (or possibly no) intervention. For an upright column, use the Irish juniper (*Juniperus communis* 'Hibernica') or *Juniperus scopulorum* 'Blue Arrow' (not 'Skyrocket', which has a tendency to die back). In a small garden, you could even use upright rosemaries, though these can be rather lax and may need tying in, possibly to a cane inserted next to the main stem, to create a strong upright. You can create obelisks by growing ivies up supports (but make sure they do not get any ideas below their station and start growing along the ground, swamping anything else that gets in their way). Use ready-made trellis obelisks or make simple bamboo wigwams (as you might for growing runner beans in the vegetable garden). Deciduous climbers can also be used – clematis and honeysuckles as well as the golden-leaved hop (*Humulus lupulus* 'Aureus'). But beware – the last is a monster.

Some evergreen shrubs are naturally ball-like, making neat domes that can be kept tight with clipping (sometimes at the expense of flowers).

*The latter cannot be clipped to a tight shape without loss of the flowers.

NATURALLY DOME-SHAPED SHRUBS AND CONIFERS

- ✓ *Chamaecyparis lawsoniana* 'Minima'
- ✓ *Choisya ternata* (Mexican orange blossom)
- ✓ *Hebe brachysiphon*
- ✓ *Hebe cupressoides* 'Boughton Dome'
- ✓ *Hebe rakaiensis*
- ✓ *Picea abies* 'Gregoryana'
- ✓ *Picea mariana* 'Nana'
- ✓ *Podocarpus nivalis*
- ✓ *Skimmia japónica*

Conifers show a wide range of form. They are unduly neglected by many designers.

Peter Anderson

Conifers

Conifers are due a revival. They have had a bad press. As suggested in Chapter 1, Alan Bloom should bear some of the responsibility for this – but only up to a point. While he rightly championed conifers as bone-hardy and low-maintenance, an awful lot of nurserymen jumped on the bandwagon and far too many conifers got marketed as 'dwarf'. A more accurate description would have been 'slow growing'. Hence many were planted in rockeries and island beds during the 1960s and 1970s, houses (with their gardens) were sold and resold, and those initially neat little shrubs are now vast trees, often dead at the base, shading out the light and sucking up moisture from the surrounding soil. Regrettably, few take kindly to hard pruning to bring them back into line.

On the positive side, conifers give a garden a sense of solidity, of permanence, just by their sheer bulk and presence. Dainty they are not (with a couple of exceptions). Many achieve a perfect shape with the minimum intervention. And they are mainly tolerant, low-maintenance plants – though they don't like strong winds very much. If you have gone down the Mediterranean route, what could be more appropriate than a well-chosen pine, cypress or juniper (alas, unless your garden is in a very favoured spot, you never get that resinous pine aroma from the first that is one of their chief attractions)? And if you're going oriental – choose a Chinese or Japanese species, of which there is a vast number.

Some have unexpected attractions. Yellow conifers, for instance, have a very fresh look in spring when the new foliage is bright and untarnished – a splendid accompaniment to other yellows provided by forsythias and daffodils, and exactly the colour you want after a cold, dark winter. Conversely, blue-leaved conifers develop their steeliest colour in a cold snap in winter. They can look splendid in isolation on a frosty lawn or with a winter mist billowing at their feet. Give some thought, therefore, to where you place them – and what you plant nearby.

Upright conifers don't take up much room – at least as young plants – and before they reach 2m can be dotted around a small garden to bring the whole design together. The Irish juniper already mentioned is dense and compact; *Juniperus scopulorum* 'Blue Arrow' is less so – though you can tie the foliage in to accentuate the vertical. They have been used with great distinction at Castle Howard in Yorkshire (admittedly a garden on the grandest scale) to give rhythm to a long border. The little dumpy conifers can drape themselves near steps. Spreading types have an unexpected use as excellent ground cover, especially on a bank, almost the ultimate low-maintenance solution. Pin the trailing stems down to the ground to persuade them to root where they come into contact with the soil. I have seen – in a garden in El Paso, where precious little would grow well, let alone flower – golden- and blue-leaved conifers planted alternately (in what might otherwise have been a herbaceous border), the main trunks ruthlessly cut back to about 45cm above ground level. Such treatment demands a certain courage, but in context was extremely convincing.

Shrubs

You are likely to be planting many more shrubs than trees – but the same criteria apply when choosing them. Always bear in mind the limitations of the site in terms of soil type and exposure to wind and cold. As a rule, deciduous shrubs are hardier than evergreens, and most hardy flowering shrubs flower during the first half of the year – from winter to late spring (the last of these being mock orange, *Philadelphus*). The ones that flower from then on – the hydrangeas and fuchsias and some others – and the evergreens tend to be slightly less hardy, and generally prefer a sheltered spot. A notable exception is the butterfly bush (*Buddleja davidii*) which will grow almost anywhere.

Shrubs with coloured leaves, or variegated leaves, need placing with care – particularly if the leaves are very thin, as on golden-leaved *Philadelphus coronarius* 'Aureus'. They need enough sun to bring out the colour (in shade, they tend to revert to plain green) but not so much that they scorch. A position where they'll be shaded from hot midday sun, by a wall, fence or tree, is best. If the garden is on acid soil, there is almost an embarrassment of choice for the late winter–spring period, as this is when the camellias and rhododendrons flower. The latter are particularly diverse, including evergreens and deciduous varieties, some (of both) being compact and mound-forming and others being more open and tree-like.

As with the trees, some shrubs have good autumn fruits. Best are the cotoneasters (red) and the pyracanthas (yellow, red or orange). *Callicarpa bodinieri* is grown almost exclusively for its berries – bright violet-purple and carried in clusters on the bare stems.

WALL SHRUBS

As discussed in Chapter 2, walls can be exploited for growing plants that would not do well in the open garden. Many shrubs of borderline hardiness – or that flower early in the year when overnight frosts can damage emerging buds in an open site – are ideal for siting in the lee of a wall. Some can be trained (formally or informally) or the wall can just be there as a backdrop. Late-flowering shrubs and evergreens often do better against a warm wall, while a north- or east-facing wall will provide shelter from wind and suits shade-loving camellias. Bear in mind that the soil at the foot of the wall will always be drier because of the rain shadow (see Chapter 2). Newly planted shrubs will need regular watering. A warm wall is the ideal spot for sun-loving ceanothus (from California), which cover themselves in blue flowers, usually in summer. They actually prefer dry soil and will revel in the heat.

This doesn't mean that every wall has to have a shrub in front of it. If the wall is in itself a thing of beauty – stone or old brick, or even brand-new but of pleasing proportions – why bother concealing it with plants? If it's predominantly shaded, there may be more mileage in painting it white or some other pale colour to reflect light.

SHRUBS FOR HOT WALLS	COMMON NAME
Acacia pravissima	Mimosa
Buddleja crispa	Himalayan butterfly bush
Callistemon	Bottlebrush
Ceanothus	California lilac
Euphorbia characias	Mediterranean spurge
Fremontodendron	
Grevillea	
Melianthus major	Honey flower
Myrtus	Myrtle
Pyracantha	Firethorn

SHRUBS FOR COOL WALLS

Camellia	
Garrya elliptica	Coast silk tassel

MASSED PLANTINGS AND GROUND COVER

An overlooked use for shrubs – and indeed for some conifers – is as ground cover. Many are suckering, producing new shoots around the base of the plant, providing excellent defence against weeds. Others have naturally lax, trailing stems that will root where they touch the ground. Pruning is a matter of shearing them over and cutting out unwanted suckers at the perimeter of the planting.

SHRUBS FOR GROUND COVER	COMMON NAME
Calluna	Heather
Cotoneaster dammeri	Bearberry cotoneaster
Erica	Heather
Gaultheria	
Hypericum calycinum	Rose of Sharon
Juniperus (prostrate forms)	Juniper
Mahonia repens	Creeping Oregon grape
Rosmarinus officinalis 'Prostratus'	Rosemary
Sarcococca	Christmas box
Thymus	Thyme
Vinca major, Vinca minor	Periwinkle

ROSES

Roses almost deserve a chapter to themselves – indeed there are a huge number of books devoted to them. Many gardeners are troubled by this group of plants' apparent needs – for pruning, feeding, pest and disease control, etc. – and it's easy to be overwhelmed by the vast number of roses available. My approach to this dangerously alluring breed is strictly pragmatic if you are considering them as a designer and/or if the requirement is for a low-maintenance garden.

First, I would ditch the old roses* – they seldom live up to the expectations engendered by their romantic names (such as 'Pompon des Princes' and 'Duchesse de Brabant'). The flowers are short-lived, usually martyrs to bad weather, the colour range is restricted (white, cream, dusky pink and carmine – no clear red, yellow or orange) and the plants themselves are often gangly, sparsely leaved and prone to disease. Such plants belong in historic gardens.

There's a very strong argument for favouring newer varieties of rose over older ones and it is to do with the way they are propagated. Rose growers are raising masses of plants annually, by grafting a tiny amount of plant material (taken from the plant they want to increase stocks of) onto rootstocks. In turn, these provide material for the succeeding generation – and so on down the years. Propagating in this way ('vegetatively' – there's no seed involved) is a bit like photo-copying a document, then taking a photocopy of the photocopy. Do this a significant number of times and there's an inevitable loss of quality and (so far as plants are concerned) vigour. Hence, rose varieties that were bred even as recently as the 1950s and 1960s – many of which are still available – are not such good plants today as they were formerly.

On that basis, I would tend to restrict choice to modern ground-cover and patio roses – bred for length of flowering season and general good health. Most of these have the advantage of bright green, glossy foliage, so the plants are always well clothed – which can't be said for all the older types. Colours include bright red, orange and yellow as well as the expected white, pink and cream. Pruning is easy – just shear them over in mid-spring (and possibly again in mid-summer, though not on those that have good autumn hips). The ones with good hips are especially useful to any designer who is looking for interest in November – producing flicks of red that will stand out against evergreen hollies, yew and box. These are excellent plants that can find a home in almost any scheme (including in containers).

Climbers

These plants are the designer's friend. Mostly fast-growing, in a year or two they will have ramped skywards up whatever support you have chosen for them. These are the head-turners of the garden. They have a multitude of uses – to cover ugly walls, outbuildings, sheds and garages, to cast their stems over pergolas to shade a walkway, over an arch that heralds the start of a path, or to ascend obelisks to add height anywhere in a scheme, possibly instead of a tree – but I would

*'Old roses' – or 'old garden roses' – is a rather inexact term, though it is accepted by most rose breeders and growers. In essence, these are plants of European origin. While some are of undoubted antiquity, most of the varieties still in cultivation were bred in the mid- to late-nineteenth century. They are further subdivided as Albas, Bourbons, Centifolias (or Provence roses), Damasks, Gallicas and Portlands (and a few others). Chinas and Teas come from further east, have a wider colour range, and they repeat flower. They are not especially robust, but cross-breeding with the old European types led to the twentieth-century hybrid teas and floribundas.

be cautious about using them on fence panels, where their weight can pull the panel down. To achieve the maximum effect in the shortest time, use annual climbers such as sweet peas (*Lathyrus odoratus*), convolvulus, Chilean glory vine (*Eccremocarpus scaber* – actually this often behaves as a perennial) or black-eyed Susan (*Thunbergia alata*).

WOODLAND HABIT

The following relates to *all* climbers. In the wild, they are plants of light woodland, where they trail around the forest floor in search of some suitable host plant to support them. Once they find one, they ramp their way up it, with astonishing vigour. Having reached the top, they spread out sideways, turning their flowers to the sun.

There are several (hidden) lessons here. One is that these are plants that will tolerate, even in some cases need, some level of shade. Against a hot wall in full sun, a climber may not do as well as you might have hoped. Conventional wisdom has it that clematis like their heads in the sun and their feet in the shade. True enough, up to a point, but this applies to all flowering climbers (including roses) and having heads in the sun may not be as necessary as you might think. Besides, against a hot wall – which intensifies the heat, as discussed in Chapter 2 – flowers bleach and fade rapidly, and the plant itself can be a martyr to mildew and other fungal diseases, especially as the soil at the foot of a wall is likely to be dry. However, for some plants, in a predominantly cool climate such as the UK's, a warm wall is essential for good flowering if not actual survival. Desirable star jasmine (*Trachelospermum jasminoides*) is a sweetly scented evergreen that must have protection from hard frost. Wisteria is perfectly hardy as a plant but flowers reliably only if the stems are baked for a period over summer – as happens when it is wall-trained. The same applies to grape vines which will grow well enough in cool areas but not ripen their fruits without sufficient heat.

CLIMBERS THAT NEED A HOT WALL	COMMON NAME
Clianthus puniceus	Parrot's bill
Eccremocarpus scaber	Chilean glory flower
Jasminum officinale	Common jasmine
Passiflora	Passion flower
Rosa banksiae 'Lutea'	Banksian rose
Solanum jasminoides 'Album'	White potato vine
Trachelospermum	Star jasmine
Wisteria	

CLIMBERS THAT TOLERATE A NORTH-FACING WALL	COMMON NAME
Clematis	
Hedera	Ivy
Hydrangea petiolaris	Climbing hydrangea
Jasminum nudiflorum	Winter-flowering jasmine
Lonicera x tellmanniana	Honeysuckle
Rosa 'Constance Spry'	'Constance Spry' rose
Rosa 'Mermaid'	'Mermaid' rose
Rosa 'Mme Alfred Carrière'	'Mme Alfred Carrière' rose
Rosa 'New Dawn'	'New Dawn' rose
Schizophragma integrifolium	Chinese hydrangea vine

Another feature of climbers, all too often overlooked, is that these are plants of great vigour with a tendency to produce strongly upright-growing stems that are sparsely clothed with leaves as they push upwards towards the light. How often have you seen in gardens climbers – particularly roses and clematis – that are a mass of bare stems (often tangled) with clusters of flowers all at the top? It is in their very nature to grow this way. From an early point of their development, therefore, stems of all climbers should be trained horizontally, ideally on wires attached to the wall or support or tied into trellis. Not only does this give better coverage, but the upward rush of growth hormones will encourage stems to push out quantities of side shoots that will be flower-bearing.

A common mistake when using climbers to cover a pergola or archway is to allow the stems to grow upright initially then spread horizontally across the top – rather as they would grow in nature, in fact. For best coverage, wrap the stems around the uprights in a spiral as they grow to encourage flower-carrying side shoots. Incidentally, when you are adding arches and pergolas to a scheme, take into account the additional thickening of the structure created by planting. In particular, allow sufficient headroom for pendulous flowers such as wisteria.

CLIMBERS WITH OTHER PLANTS

You can also use climbers to add interest (dare I say colour?) to a massed planting of shrubs that had their moment of glory in spring. Late-flowering clematis planted among them are ideal for this purpose.* Cut them hard back in late winter before the shrubs get going. These will flower while the clematis are just starting into growth. Simply allow the flexible clematis stems to find their own way through the shrubs – they will flower later in the year. The annual climbers mentioned above can be used in the same way, especially if it's necessary to introduce late colour into an established planting that presents as a sea of green in summer.

This can be taken to romantic, even absurd, lengths. Climbing roses driven into the arms of an existing (and no longer fully productive) apple tree look voluptuous when in full flower (as also do wisteria and small-flowered clematis). Once established, these plantings appear guileless and relaxed – because formal pruning and training in this instance is not practical – and give a garden a look of wild abandon. But it's easy to get carried away with this idea and to start freely planting climbers to launch themselves into any tree, shrubbery or conifer. I have seen tall conifers embraced by rambler roses and vigorous – it just does not look right, rather as though it is the conifer itself that has put out flowers. Nevertheless, nothing creates quite such a sense of abundance as an established climber covered in flowers.

It's critical to match the vigour of the two plants. In particular, the host plant should already be well established, or the newcomer will impede its progress. An established host plant, however, will be sucking up most of the available moisture from the soil it occupies. The climber should be planted a good distance away from it – at least a metre. I learnt this the hard way, by planting the delightful (but scentless) orange honeysuckle *Lonicera* x *tellmanniana* too close to an old apple tree. After fifteen years, it has finally made its way to the upper canopy and now does what was required. Shafts of light that filter down through the tree's canopy now illuminate the still somewhat sparse flowers during its brief – but keenly anticipated – season.

*Clematis are normally divided into three groups depending on the flowering season. Group 1 comprises those that flower between late winter and late spring (the last of these being the vigorous *Clematis montana*). Group 2 – of which there is only a small number – have two flushes of flowers, in late spring to early summer, then again from mid- to late summer. (Some varieties produce double flowers in the first flush.) Group 3 is the largest group, flowering from mid-summer to autumn.

CHOOSING PLANTS FOR THE GARDEN: PERENNIALS, ANNUALS AND BULBS

When planting trees (especially) and shrubs as discussed in the previous chapter, your eye is always on the longer term – these are plants that may well outlive you (or your client). They are a permanent presence, contributing to the scene year-round. It's usual to fill in the framework they create with soft-stemmed, lower-growing plants – perennials, annuals and bulbs. Shorter-lived and faster-growing (usually), these often give immediate results or at least reach maturity in a relatively short time. These are the plants that fill beds and borders with colour, mainly in spring and summer, often overflowing the edges of beds and borders and softening lines that would otherwise be clean.

In a sense, we are talking about the jam on the bread. While trees and shrubs provide shape and structure – volumes and voids – soft-stemmed plants are grown mainly for their flowers, usually colourful. In most cases, these flowers are presented at waist level or below, though some of these plants hug the ground or rise as tall as shrubs. There is a much wider colour range available within this group of plants than within the woody ones. Talking of volumes and voids, these plants can be a fundamental element in the dynamics or rhythm of a garden. Imagine a scheme that in winter comprises a mix of related – or, for that matter, unrelated – shapes, then the contrast as these merge and integrate with an infill of spring and summer plants.

Unlike certain trees and shrubs, most of the plants under discussion here are not particular about soil pH. However, soil texture remains an issue, and whatever type you are working with will have an impact on what you will be able to plant. Aspect continues to be important in guiding your choice. If you read in a plant catalogue or dictionary that a plant can be grown in both sun and shade, interpret it as follows:

- Plants will flower more freely in sun, but the flowers will fade more quickly than in shade, and the colour may bleach rapidly.
- Plants in full sun will be better in slightly heavy soil that does not dry out too much in summer.

Colour Theory

This is a hurdle that you need to vault – and move on from. Many gardeners are obsessed with colour – and, but to a lesser extent, form and texture – taking a painterly approach that they allow to override the needs of particular plants. In other words, they choose and combine plants solely on the basis of flower colour. But this is not really what design is about and to some extent represents part of a historical trend. As with baroque ornaments, you should be able to strip them away and still find good design beneath. A well-designed sofa, strategically placed in a beautifully proportioned room, remains a well-designed sofa no matter how many cushions and throws you fling over it. Besides, the plants themselves should integrate, irrespective of flower colour. Or, if they do not integrate, it should be in the interests of design.*

We identify three primary colours – the ones that can't be created by mixing others: red, yellow and blue. The complementary colour of any of these is created by combining the other two:

PRIMARY COLOUR	COMPLEMENTARY COLOUR
Red	Green (yellow + blue)
Yellow	Purple (blue + red)
Blue	Orange (red + yellow)

*For instance, if you place a series of phormiums, with strongly upright, sword-like leaves, among low ground cover. In this case, you are treating them less as plants but more as sculptures. From the southern hemisphere, phormiums always have a foreign look to them in UK gardens.

They are sometimes presented in a wheel arrangement. Richard Of York Gave Battle In Vain is a commonly used mnemonic to navigate your way round the wheel (going clockwise) – red, orange, yellow, green, blue, indigo, violet. (Actually, forget indigo, which is merely blue under another name.)

Complementary colours play a particular role in design – especially graphic design. The effect of a primary colour in combination with its complementary colour is striking – the two seem to pulsate (as an example, imagine red type on a green background – it is eyeball-bruising). They are not, in any sense, harmonious. These colours lie opposite each other on a

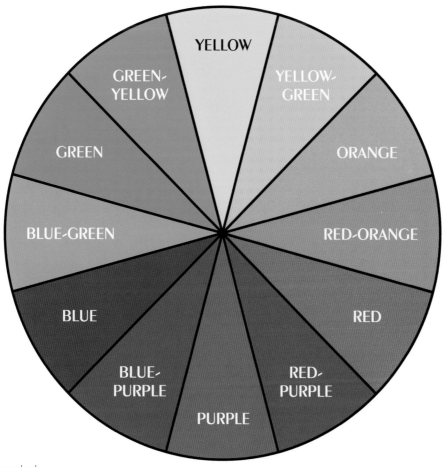

The colour wheel

colour wheel.* Colours that lie next to each other (and are adjacent in the above sequence) are usually considered harmonious – blue and lilac, for instance, or yellow and orange. (But note also that red and purple, and blue and purple lie next to each other, which is where this 'theory' starts to break down. They seldom look good in combination. The purple border at Sissinghurst is famously sombre.) So, for a harmonious planting, choose colours (and shades of colours, such as lilac, pink and cream) that lie next to one another, using complementaries for a more exciting effect. For instance, tulips and wallflowers or forget-me-nots are a classic spring combination. Orange tulips would harmonize with yellow wallflowers but would create quite a different impression with blue forget-me-nots. One of the most frequently photographed examples of complementaries used on the large scale was at Rosemary Verey's garden at Barnsley, near Cirencester. Here, an avenue of yellow-flowered laburnums, trained as a tunnel, supported purple wisteria, the two flowering simultaneously. At their feet were mauve alliums. The whole scheme was deliberately contrived. Its strength lay in the contrast between the strict observance of regular planting and restriction of colour as opposed to the lushness of the flowers.

In practice – and you read it here first – colour theory has limited application in the garden. For one thing, many flower colours are not true. While there are plenty of yellows and oranges, clear reds are few, most veering towards the purple (i.e. have some blue in them). Equally, there are precious few blues – most flowers described as blue are actually purple, with a greater or lesser degree of red in them. And while blue and purple, according to the theory, harmonize, the combination is dreary. Moreover, many flowers have more than one colour in them – for instance, a purple iris may be marked with yellow, white and brown, and roses often change colour as they progress from the bud stage to the open flower.

Additionally, in any planting, it is impossible to eliminate the colour green. Red- and pink-flowered plants always create some degree of impact simply because they have green leaves.

Mix all the colours and what you get is not – as many assume – a sludgy brown, but a severe, gunmetal grey. Combined with any of the colours, grey will read as its complementary. Red lettering on a grey background makes for a similar effect to red on green – it seems that the eye picks up on the green in the grey. Thus grey too should be used with caution in any planting – contrary to received opinion, it isn't necessarily a soothing background presence, but can make a possibly unintended impact. Grey-leaved foliage plants such as *Senecio cineraria* 'Silver Dust' are commonly used in gardenesque park bedding schemes as an edging. Next time you come across this, just note what effect it has on the nearby flower colours.

---

*Incidentally – and perhaps surprisingly – these colour combinations have exactly the same impact on people who have some degree of colour blindness, even if they cannot identify the colours precisely.

WHITE

There's one almost unavoidable colour not dealt with thus far, and which by convention does not appear on the wheel – white. This is the most dominant of all the colours, as it reflects the maximum amount of light. Because of this, white objects always appear slightly bigger than they actually are – almost as though they have a halo. This is an effect you'll notice particularly at dusk, when the whites suddenly loom out of the gathering darkness.* It's commonly assumed that a planting comprising white – or pale pastel – flowers must necessarily be 'soothing'. It isn't.

White should be used with caution next to complementaries. It kills the force of these stone dead, and the eye finds no resting place. As an example, picture that much-anticipated event of early spring, the flowering of the crocuses. Great carpets of colour suddenly brighten up the scene. Crocus bulbs are often sold cheap in autumn as bulk mixtures of yellow, white and purple for mass planting in lawns. But when they all appear together, the effect is 'busy', even sickly. Try weeding out one of the colours to leave just two. Yellow and purple will be very strong (they are complementaries), yellow and white rather fresh, while purple and white will look cool. All three together, and they make no impact at all (or a very messy one).

Vita Sackville-West must shoulder the blame for creating a white garden at Sissinghurst (though admittedly her description of planting it is very romantic and evocative) – a planting that comprises nothing but white-flowered plants.** Apart from the 'looming' issue discussed above, the problem with white-flowered plants *en masse* is that so few are truly white. Many veer towards cream or pink, and can even look dirty when placed next to chalkier whites. Besides, many white flowers are flushed or marked with other colours. The most successful white planting I have seen was in a garden divided into 'rooms' (as indeed is Sissinghurst). In early June, the combination of ivory roses ('Iceberg'), white peonies and white foxgloves with straw-coloured *Astrantia major* and glaucous *Hosta sieboldiana* was at its peak, and attendant green foliage was still fresh-looking. The effect cannot have been remotely as good later in the season.

Perennials

A perennial is a soft-stemmed plant that lives for three or more years. Some, such as peonies and hellebores, can live a lot longer than that and are often concomitantly slow-growing. There are some that tend to become woody with age, such as asters and chrysanthemums, and these usually need to be replaced fairly regularly with younger, more productive specimens. Fresh

*A brief note on dark colours (there are no truly black plants). If white and very pale colours loom, darks do the opposite – they recede. This has limited applications as far as flowering plants are concerned, as there are so few with truly dark flowers.

**This was not the first example. Gertrude Jekyll made a couple of white gardens, but these never achieved the same level of fame.

Many of the late-flowering perennials are daisies in the yellow-orange-red colour range – such as this rudbeckia.

Ernst Benary Samenzucht GmbH

growth appears at the edge of the plant, with the middle part becoming progressively bare. The majority of hardy perennials flower from late spring and into summer, with a few continuing thereafter into autumn. Most perennials die back completely over winter ('herbaceous perennials'), leaving you with possibly extensive tracts of bare earth. (If you are creating a border for a friend or professionally for a client, you may have to reassure them that the plants have not died and will indeed return the following year.) There are a precious few evergreen or semi-evergreen perennials. These are valued for providing some green over winter but they can, however, look a bit tatty if frosted. By and large, perennials are reliable and unfussy plants. They are the essential component of prairie plantings and many schemes that demand a low-maintenance solution.

EVERGREEN PERENNIALS	COMMON NAME
Arum italicum 'Pictum'	
Bergenia	Elephant's ears
Epimedium	
Euphorbia myrsinites	
Helleborus	Hellebore
Hemerocallis (some)	Daylily
Ophiopogon	
Phormium	New Zealand flax
Saxifraga (some)	Saxifrage
Stachys lanata	Bunnies' ears

But while perennials may be above ground for several months, flowering occurs (usually) over only a few weeks. That leaves you with quite a lot of green to take account of in your design – of the new foliage before they have flowered, then with the foliage afterwards. Hence the problem attendant on schemes based solely around flower colour is that the planned effect will occur only during a specific window. Some perennials, however, have interesting foliage that can be a good foil to other plants, or indeed make its own mark. A few are grown exclusively for their foliage – the flowers are either incidental or a distraction (indeed can even be removed).

PERENNIALS WITH GOOD FOLIAGE   COMMON NAME

Bergenia . . . . Elephant's ears
Helleborus . . . . Hellebore
Heuchera
Hosta
Iris
Paeonia . . . . Peony
Rheum. . . . . Ornamental rhubarb
Tellima
Thalictrum

Ernst Benary Samenzucht GmbH

Spring-flowering bergenias make excellent evergreen ground
cover in sun or partial shade – and are tolerant of poor soils.

PERENNIALS FOR GROUND COVER

One of the most important uses of perennials is to provide ground cover – weed-suppressing vegetation that presents as a carpet of green over a long period. If they flower, so much the better. If you are looking for a low-maintenance solution for an expanse of ground, these plants fit the bill. Note that ground-cover plants do not need to be evergreen – many form impenetrable mats of roots just below ground level, effectively choking out competing weeds even when the soil is bare. In spring and summer, the dense topgrowth will prevent weed seeds from hitting the soil and germinating. A few well-chosen plants in quantity arranged in great interlocking drifts often provide an easy solution where any large expanse of ground has to be filled, and this is the principle that informs much of latter-day 'low-maintenance' design.

A feature of most ground-cover plants, however, is that they are often fast-growing and potentially invasive – to the extent that they can become weeds themselves. However, if you are determined to avoid a sweep of gravel over a membrane, they offer an ideal (green in all senses) solution. They are not maintenance-free, however – you will have to weed between young plants until they have spread and merged together, and once established they will need management. But most are easily kept in check by shearing over the topgrowth once or twice a year and digging out any new plants that appear at the edge and threaten to extend the spread too wide.

PERENNIALS FOR GROUND COVER	COMMON NAME
Ajuga reptans	Bugle
Alchemilla mollis	Lady's mantle
Bergenia	Elephant's ears
Campanula glomerata	Clustered bellflower
Convallaria majalis	Lily-of-the-valley
Epimedium	
Euphorbia amygdaloides var. *robbiae*	Wood spurge
Euphorbia cyparissias	Cypress spurge
Geranium	
Heuchera	
Hosta	
Hypericum	
Lamium	Dead-nettle
Pachysandra terminalis	Japanese spurge
Polygonum bistorta	Bistort
Polystichum setiferum	Soft-shield fern
Tiarella cordifolia	Foam flower
Vinca	Periwinkle

GRASSES

Historically, grasses were not much used in garden design until the mid-twentieth century – since then they have gained in popularity to the point where they have become almost a cliché.

Ernst Benary Samenzucht GmbH

With steely blue leaves, *Festuca glauca* is widely used as a gap-filler.

Small wonder. Alan Bloom was partly responsible, combining them in shapely combinations with conifers and heathers. Generally colonizing plants, in nature they often consolidate tracts of ground (both wet and dry, depending on the species) and provide a valuable habitat for all manner of wildlife. They are perhaps the ultimate low-maintenance plant, rapidly forming dense, weed-suppressing blankets, and are essential in any Piet Oudolf-inspired prairie planting (see Chapter 1). Ecologists love them. There are grasses suitable for all soil types, sun or shade, evergreen and herbaceous (with some annuals) and most are very quick-growing. Flowering takes place over a long period, and the seed heads that follow, persisting into winter, add to their perceived attractions. Colours are in the subdued range, however – at best a pinkish, creamy or silvery beige. Their value has perhaps been exaggerated. Admittedly, they can be used to mitigate a potential colour clash between neighbouring plants, but I do not entirely endorse the view that they bring 'movement' to the garden, as breezes blow through their silken flower heads – or that this must somehow be desirable.

That said, some gardeners are unreasonably prejudiced against pampas grass (*Cortaderia selloana*), simply on the grounds of its ubiquity (and suburban connotations, along with decking, conifers and heathers). It has its uses. But this is a plant of very distinctive outline – a mound of leaves that cascade outwards topped by tall feathery plumes. As a specimen in a lawn, it can be cliché.

FERNS

Ferns are unduly neglected – perhaps because they do not flower. But the fronds are slug-proof and seemingly immune to disease. While some are evergreen, many die back over winter. At their best, they are shapely and elegant, if understated. Nearly all ferns are best in shade, in soil that is reliably damp (as it often is in such situations). In a cool, shady courtyard, try combining them with plants of similar needs – Japanese maples and hostas, with attendant mosses and lichens. Handsomest of all, the Japanese painted fern (*Athyrium nipponicum* var. *pictum*) needs acid soil.

OASE (UK) Ltd

Many designers are keen on grasses – they fill space and look good over a long period.

Ferns can be extremely architectural. Best of all in this respect are so-called tree ferns (*Dicksonia antarctica*), which have a tall fibrous trunk topped by spreading fronds. They became extremely popular towards the end of the twentieth century. A drawback is that they are so slow-growing – the trunk extends only by about 2.5cm per year – so to make any kind of impact, it's necessary to plant a fairly mature specimen. The age of large plants is reflected in the price – they are usually very expensive. More to the point, these are plants of high-altitude cloud forests and seldom look at home in most gardens – plus the uppermost parts are vulnerable to frosts. Place them with care.

TENDER PERENNIALS

There is a group of plants loosely referred to as 'tender perennials' that have quite distinct uses in design. These are plants that, while being perennial (in the sense outlined previously), will not withstand frost. They can only be used as part of a permanent scheme in frost-free gardens, such as you may find near the coast. Most familiar in this group are pelargoniums and osteospermums, to which can be added felicias, diascias and heliotropes. Strangely, they are nearly all of South African origin.

They are generally treated as half-hardy annuals (see p. 91). Their chief value lies in the speed with which they grow and the freedom of their flowering – over a long period and usually right up to the first frosts. They are excellent for use in summer containers, combined with annuals.

Annuals (and biennials)

An annual is a plant that completes its growth cycle within a calendar year. Seed is sown in late winter to spring, the plants flower in summer, set seed, then die. It's a short life, but a productive one – they are usually in flower over a much longer period than perennials and shrubs, and many cover themselves with flowers to the extent that the leaves are no longer visible.

Many designers – in fact, many gardeners – are under the illusion that a biennial lives for two years. This isn't strictly true. Biennials are sown in summer/autumn and the little plants overwinter for flowering the following spring – hence the growth cycle is still completed within twelve months.* Obviously, annuals and biennials can play no part in permanent plantings, but they are extremely useful in the short term and almost essential if you are looking to provide colour in late summer.

*In other words, annuals and biennials are the same thing (as the plants can hardly know it's Christmas) and they have a similar use in garden design. It's possible to make a late sowing of hardy annuals that – if overwintered under cover – will flower the following spring. Equally, some biennials will flower the same year, if you make an early enough sowing.

One thing is inescapable. These plants represent hard work. Unless you buy bedding plants from a nursery or garden centre, you have to invest time in raising the plants yourself from seed (possibly under cover). Frequent deadheading is important once they are planted, to encourage continuous flowering.

HARDY AND HALF-HARDY

Annuals are described as hardy or half-hardy – an important distinction. Hardy annuals will withstand freezing temperatures, so can be planted out (or even sown outdoors) in mid- to late spring for flowering come the start of summer. Half-hardy annuals have to be protected from frost until freezing conditions are no longer expected (this is often later in the year than you would imagine – wonderful warm sunny days in May are often followed by freezing nights). It's worth pointing this out, as half-hardy annuals are commonly sold as bedding plants in garden

Gazanias are annuals of southern African origin that open their flowers only in full sun.

centres throughout spring, and it's easy to make a mistake and include them in a planting only for them to succumb to night frosts. Planting of half-hardies should be left till June in most parts of the country.

USING ANNUALS

The high value of annuals lies in the abundance of flowers – and hence colour – provided over a long period. They are invaluable to any gardener who needs to fill a space (reasonably) cheaply in a short space of time. They are ideal for filling in gaps between young shrubs and perennials that need time to spread and achieve the intended effect. If the gaps are planted with annuals, not only do you create the impression of a more established planting, but you reduce the risk of weeds germinating.

You can also leave parts of the garden unplanted to permit you to experiment with different annuals in subsequent years (if you are working for a client, the brief may allow for this). This gives you the opportunity to play with different colour combinations, so the garden is never the same two years running. Any particularly effective scheme can always be rendered permanent by the use of perennials in the same colour range. Such is received opinion, anyway. But many annual varieties have been bred for intensity of colour – colour that you may struggle to find among the frequently more subdued perennials.

An important use of annuals is in containers, windowboxes and hanging baskets. If you have planted the garden for low maintenance, with a mix of hardy perennials, grasses and shrubs, you will almost certainly find that colour is in short supply towards the end of summer. A few large containers planted with annuals (and tender perennials), strategically placed, will give the impression of a still floriferous garden – the permanent plants will act as a backdrop.

An unexpected use of annuals is as instant, quick-growing temporary ground cover.

Bulbs

Bulbs – I use the term loosely* – are actually perennials, but they have evolved a special mechanism that allows them to go dormant when conditions are unfavourable for growth (usually when it's hot and dry in summer or freezing cold in winter). The bulb, usually swollen and sometimes fleshy, acts as a storage organ. In practical terms, this means bulbs are above ground for a much shorter period of time than other perennials. They produce their topgrowth and flowers often in a matter of weeks, then die back again. Unlike other perennials, though, they tend not to spread – their habit is strictly vertical. They are nearly always sold as bare bulbs during the dormant period, so their use has to be planned for – it is not practical (besides being prohibitively expensive) to plant them as growing plants.

While there's a bulb for virtually every season, the vast majority – at least so far as hardy bulbs are concerned – are plants of spring. Spring bulbs appear in a sequence – snowdrops, winter aconites** and crocuses (appearing at the back end of winter) give way to daffodils, tulips and hyacinths. They add much to the rhythm of a garden: viewed as a group, they become bigger and more richly coloured in line with the lengthening and increased warmth of the days. Low-growing, the first three are excellent in patches to break up an expanse of bare earth around shrubs and trees or as informal drifts.

Daffodils (*Narcissus*), the largest group, are the most variable of the spring bulbs. There are literally hundreds of varieties, some flowering as early as late winter, while others will coincide with the tulips in mid- to late spring. While flower colour is restricted to white, cream and yellow (sometimes touched with orange, and there are a couple of pink varieties), flower size varies considerably. Some are graceful and elegant, others much more robust (even coarse). Be wary

*Really, one should speak of 'bulbs, corms and tubers', but it's useful to lump them all together as bulbs, as they all behave in the same way and have similar uses in the garden.

**Unlike most other bulbs, both snowdrops and aconites are best planted not as bare bulbs but as growing plants (in storage, the bare bulbs dry out too much). They are often sold mail order – check advertisements in the gardening press – in early spring, after plants have flowered but before they have died back.

of sacks of mixed daffodils, therefore. It is not that these are not of good quality – but you will find that not only do they not all flower at the same time, but flower size and colour will also vary accordingly. For an integrated look with a predictable flowering time, plant quantities of a single variety.

Early bulbs are also excellent in drifts or clumps beneath deciduous trees and shrubs. They are above ground while the branches overhead are still bare, so they have plenty of access to light and rainfall. By the time the permanent plants are in leaf (and casting a heavy shade with a canopy that also keeps the ground too dry for most plants), they will be experiencing their summer dormancy. Some of the later spring bulbs are natural woodlanders and actually prefer dappled shade. In a planting of native trees or an orchard, nothing could be more appropriate than carpets of English bluebells* – but do not overlook camassias, the North American equivalent. These have spires of starry flowers of a smoky blue not found in any other plant.

Several early bulbs, especially crocuses, some daffodils and snake's-head fritillaries (*Fritillaria meleagris*), can be used for naturalizing in lawns – an easy way of creating a 'meadow' look without all the hard work (see also Chapter 6). For the longevity of the bulbs, you can't mow until all the foliage has died back below ground – in other words, until the bulbs have completed their growth cycle. Either delay mowing until after they have died back (usually six to eight weeks after flowering) or mow round individual clumps. The last of the bulbs that are suitable for such informal schemes is a dainty wild gladiolus (*Gladiolus byzantinus*), with luminous magenta flowers.

Early bulbs are also effectively used to add early colour to beds planted with later-flowering herbaceous perennials. The bulbs will emerge and flower while the perennials are still dormant (or only just coming into growth). The emerging foliage will effectively conceal the fading leaves of the bulbs as they die back.

Late-spring tulips and hyacinths are much more sophisticated. More evidently hybrids than any of the above, they have flowers in often very saturated colours, and are excellent for providing a colour 'hit' in massed plantings. Their thick-textured flowers do not generally integrate well with other plants, though a traditional use of tulips combines them with spring biennials such as wallflowers or forget-me-nots – albeit in formal schemes. In fact, it is best to deal with their air of artificiality head on. They are mostly at their best when standing stiffly to attention in geometric beds and large containers. And while the earlier bulbs are plants for the longer term – they can be planted then left *in situ* for an annual comeback – these more highly bred bulbs

*Be sure to plant the English bluebell (*Hyacinthoides non-scripta*), with flowers of a distinct indigo, not the Spanish one. The latter (*Hyacinthoides hispanica*) is a coarser plant with larger, paler blue flowers that will hybridize with (and eventually dominate) the native bluebell, if given the chance. While it's illegal to collect bulbs from the wild, specialist suppliers sell guaranteed seed-raised plants, often sold in full leaf after flowering, like snowdrops and winter aconites.

are rarely so good in subsequent years. They are best discarded after flowering and replaced with fresh bulbs each year.

Reliable summer bulbs are relatively few and far between. Alliums (ornamental onions) are expensive but have one very desirable characteristic (in the eyes of some designers). The flowers are held in perfectly spherical heads of a precision unequalled by most other plants. Added to this almost artificial appearance, colours include a metallic blue and an electric violet. Almost inevitably, they convey a sense of artifice to any planting. Placed at regular intervals to rise above billowing perennials, they will introduce a (temporary) note of formality. Unlike nearly all the other bulbs, the seed heads retain the shape of the flower head, and can be allowed to remain till autumn.

Lilies (*Lilium*) comprise a somewhat larger, more variable group of plants. Some have very particular needs as to soil type and vary in tolerance of sun and shade. There are several species as well as many hybrids with large flowers, some heavily scented (a few overpoweringly so). Shade-tolerant types are woodland plants, making an excellent addition to a cool planting of deciduous shrubs. The hybrids (and thick-petalled species such as *Lilium regale*) are more glamorous, deserving a prominent position for their sculptural quality and brevity of flowering. Many are best grown in isolation in large containers.

That leaves gladioli and dahlias for the end of the growing season. Gladioli are excellent for solid, saturated colour (if you can deal with their stiff, artificial appearance), while dahlias are in flower for longer than any of the other bulbs. Neither of these are low-maintenance, however. They need staking as they grow and the bulbs have to be lifted and stored after flowering (or discarded) – they are hardy only in the most favoured gardens.

LAWNS…AND OTHER GREEN SURFACES

A lawn is often a major constituent of a garden – an expanse of green that can be used for a number of purposes. It may be multi-functional, serving as an area for sunbathing and relaxing, children's games or maybe just for hanging out the washing. On an aesthetic level, as a flat surface it acts as a contrast to more mounded, uneven plantings of shrubs and perennials. In a formal scheme of strict proportions, it is often the horizontal plane from which vertical hedges and other elements rise up at right angles. Chances are, however, that the lawn will see a lot of heavy use.

Contrary to what you might think, it is always easier (and cheaper) to revive an existing lawn, however neglected, than to make one from scratch (see 'Restoring a neglected lawn', p. 101). All lawns benefit from attention now and again. If you are working on a garden professionally, in whatever capacity, you can make this part of the brief even if the client has not given any thought to the present state of the grass. While a lawn is high-maintenance, needing much more than a regular mow, grass can also be very forgiving – standing up well to wear and tear (if properly maintained) and easily brought back into commission if it has got out of hand.

Planning

When you're planning a lawn, think not only of the use it will be put to but how easy it will be to maintain it. Steps up to a lawn are all very well, but how are you going to get the lawnmower up them? You may need to devise a separate sloping service path in that scenario – discreetly hidden, if it does not form part of the design.

Very small lawns – less than 3m square – are not worth the trouble. Unless strictly ornamental (i.e. no one is expected to set foot on them), even light use will wear them out rapidly. Grass paths running round island beds, in the Alan Bloom style, should also ideally be 3m wide if they are not to become rivers of mud during a wet summer.

Grass always does best in full sun. It's possible to make a lawn in a lightly shaded site (around an airy, deciduous tree, for instance), but you will have to choose a grass type that's shade tolerant. In a garden that's heavily shaded by evergreen trees, walls and fences or hedges, you may well need to find an alternative.

Seed vs turf

You can either grow a lawn from seed or lay turf in strips. Choice will be guided by what time of year you are making the lawn and your budget, balanced against how quickly you want a usable surface. Longer term, it's impossible to tell the difference between a lawn made from turf and one grown from seed – they look the same. Unless very rigorously maintained, both will be pushing up daisies and other lawn weeds within the same space of time. As most of us are impatient, chances are you'll be laying turf – but it's worth saying something about seed, as the preparation of the site is the same either way. You may in any case be using seed to make a wildflower meadow – see below.

Sowing seed is a more versatile option than laying turf, as there is a wider choice of seed mixes available – hardwearing types that suit family gardens, low-maintenance mixes (of slower-growing grasses that need less frequent mowing), as well as mixes for fine lawns, drought and shade and for overseeding existing lawns (for more on overseeding, see 'Restoring a neglected lawn', on p. 101). A seed-sown lawn will need a year or two before you can subject it to typical use. During the first year, foot traffic should be restricted to mowing. Sowing seed, however, is always a cheaper option than laying turf, and may well be easier if you are dealing with a large area. A disadvantage is that many types can only be sown at particular times of year, ideally during periods of damp weather in autumn or spring. Modern mixes can also be sown in summer, but there's a greater risk of the seedling grasses scorching in hot, dry periods.

For an instant lawn, lay turf. This looks good straight away, and is usable within a matter of weeks. Turf can be laid at any time, except if the ground is frozen or waterlogged, and during a hot, dry spell in summer it isn't a good idea either. The best time is autumn or late winter – a generally cool time of year when the turf is least likely to dry out and shrink after laying. It can also successfully be laid in spring and summer, but regular watering will probably be needed in the ensuing weeks – something for the maintenance contract, if you are working professionally.

Turf is obviously convenient and is usually very quick to lay – rather like a laminate floor, but easier as the material is soft and flexible. The downside is that you're under something of a time constraint. Turf is cut from a field, rolled up (grass side inwards), then delivered to the retail outlet – and this is how you buy it, in rolls. As they're starved of light, the blades of grass rapidly turn yellow. At the same time, the sod begins to dry out and can crack. Ideally, you'll start laying the grass as soon as it arrives on site. If you have to wait for a few days for any reason, unroll it (if you can) and give it a light sprinkle. Roll it back up, and put the rolls in a cool, shady area, covered loosely with heavy-duty plastic to prevent further drying out. If you can't unroll it – difficult in a confined space – lightly hose over the rolls as they are, then top with plastic.

Bearing in mind the cost of turf, it pays to be very accurate when calculating the area you wish to cover. While you need to have enough, excess cannot easily be disposed of, apart from as an expensive addition to the compost heap.

Site preparation

At the risk of stating the obvious, a lawn should be as perfectly flat as you can manage (or maybe have a very gentle, even slope). Otherwise, it will be difficult to mow.

Dig over the site and clear it of all perennial weeds, large stones and rubble. If you're doing the job in mid-spring, applying a weedkiller to any green growth a week or so before you start (if possible) is not at all a bad idea. If you're doing the job in winter, pay particular attention to weed roots – any scrap left behind will carry on growing. This is a strong argument for making a lawn in spring, when you can identify the weeds.

Now is the time to carry out any necessary soil improvement. Dig in grit if you know the drainage is poor, fork in a general garden fertilizer and add some garden compost (if you have it) or other soil improver (avoiding farmyard manure, unless treated, which itself is likely to contain weed seeds). Tread or lightly roller the soil to level it (a good test of how much you have improved the structure – if mud sticks to your boots, more grit is needed), then rake over, in both directions, to create a lovely crumbly tilth.

Ideally, you then get on with other tasks, leaving the ground to rest for around ten days. This allows for any dormant weed seeds that you've brought to the surface during cultivation to germinate – you can then hoe them off. It also allows the ground to 'settle' – so you can review the level and fill in any slightly sunken areas before sowing or laying the turf.

This is something of a luxury, however, and chances are that you'll need to get on with making the lawn itself.

MOWING STRIPS

This is a matter of common sense, but it's easily forgotten. When planning any lawn, you have to give some consideration to how easy it will be to mow. If the lawn adjoins flower beds, edging it with a line of bricks or pavers will allow you to maintain a neat edge without mowing into any plants. Equally, if the lawn meets a wall, run a line of bricks (or gravel) between the wall and the edge of the lawn. While a mowing strip may not be visible at all times of year (it may be disguised by planting in summer), it should form an integral part of the design. Use a sympathetic material that will be in tune with other hard landscaping in the garden – or introduce a deliberate contrast.

Sowing seed

For really accurate sowing, mark out the area with a grid into metre squares using stakes and twine (for more information on marking out a site, see Chapter 9). The soil should be damp when you sow, to ensure good adhesion between the seed and the soil surface. If the ground looks dry, give it a quick (but thorough) hose down, with the sprinkler on a fine setting. The rate at which the seed should be sown is indicated on the seed packet (or box). It's worth weighing out the first square metre's worth, then sowing this, so you can get a feel of how thickly to sow. Even sowing is actually quite important – but it's better to sow thinly rather than too thickly (somewhat counter-intuitively). If the coverage is too thin, you can always scatter more seed over later. But sow too thick and the seedlings will be crowded, competing with each other for light. They will not grow strongly – and thinning them will be a pain.

As with buttering bread, be sure that seed is evenly distributed right to the edges. After scattering, lightly rake over the whole area, just to cover the seed. Ideally, stand outside the seeded area and reach in with the rake to avoid walking on the soil. Germination is usually brisk – within one to two weeks. It's important during these initial stages that the ground does not dry out, so be prepared to sprinkle over the site if the weather is dry to keep the seedlings growing strongly.

Once the seedlings are 5cm tall, lightly roller over them, if you can. As mad as this sounds, it's an important part of establishing the lawn. Rollering consolidates the soil around the roots so that, when you give the grass its first cut (a light one, a couple of days after rollering), the mower is much less likely to rip the seedlings out of the ground. Don't worry too much about flattening the seedlings with the roller – they will soon get over it.

Laying turf

If you want to know how to lay turf, the short, if facetious, answer is – grass side up. There really is not much more to it.

Starting at one end, unroll the first strip. You need to move forwards into the lawn as you work so as not to tread on the prepared soil (which would ruin the structure) – so you'll need to position yourself outside the proposed area when laying the first strip. (This is the opposite to the way you would lay a laminate floor, where it's usual to work backwards, into the room.) Cut off the excess at the end with a sharp knife. Gently tamp down the strip with the head of a rake held vertically. Now you can lay a plank on the strip to kneel on while you lay the next strip (the plank spreads your weight). Start the second strip with the excess cut from the first roll, then start a new roll.

Be methodical when laying the strips. Always start at the same side and work in the same direction (e.g. left to right, always starting from the left side, or vice versa). This achieves a cleaner finish and ensures that the cut marks between consecutive strips are evenly distributed across the lawn.

Butt each new strip up as tightly as you can to the preceding one, using the back of the rake or your hand. Don't be cautious about this – you need to lay as tight as possible to guard against shrinkage. Continue until the lawn is laid. Finally, topdress the lawn with a mix of lawn sand and (if you have any) garden compost or a soil improver, brushed over with a stiff lawn brush.

Newly laid turf won't stand much traffic until the strips have knitted together. In mild, damp weather, this can happen in as little as a couple of weeks. If the weather stays warm and dry, water it regularly. If it does start to dry out (or if you do find you have laid the lawn too loosely) and tell-tale lines open up between the strips, all is not lost. Just fill in the gaps with a mix of potting compost and sand, then sow some grass seed over it.

The lawn is usable after six to eight weeks. Give it a light trim after a few weeks, if it's growing strongly.

Round, oval and irregular shapes

It is a straightforward matter to cut an existing lawn to a new shape. If you wish to make a round, oval or irregularly shaped lawn from scratch, it is easiest to do so using turf.

To create a circular lawn, lay the turf in strips, progressively longer then shorter (as if to make a rough diamond shape), slightly exceeding the intended final area. Ideally, allow a period of weeks for the turf to establish before proceeding. Mark the centre of the circle by knocking a stake into the turf at that point. Attach a string to the stake. Measure the radius of the circle against the string and mark it on the string with a knot or blob of paint. Get hold of a can of spray paint and in the same hand grasp the string at the marked point. Pull the string taut, then, keeping the can close to the ground (to create a clear line), move around in a circle, spraying the turf as you go. Cut out the circle with a half-moon edger. Incidentally, have no fear about the paint on the grass being permanent. As with hair dye, it will grow out.

For an oval, mark two overlapping circles of different sizes, then run a thick rope or length of hosepipe around them as a guide before cutting. An irregular kidney shape is most easily done by eye. Lay a length of rope or hose on the ground and adjust it until you have the desired shape. Hold it in position with a number of stakes or tent pegs.*

Staying with lawns, you can visually reduce the size of a large lawn by marking a circle within it. Cut out a narrow strip and replace this with bricks, cobbles or gravel just to break up a large expanse of green or define an area within it – perhaps to be used for entertaining. This can also be a useful strategy for strengthening the design in a garden where the lawn is – possibly for practical reasons – proportionally too large, perhaps in relation to an adjacent patio.

ALTERNATIVES TO GRASS

There are several alternatives to a traditional grass lawn if a soft area is required. In some cases, however, it may be advisable to consider hard landscaping instead (including decking), as discussed in the following chapter.

CHAMOMILE

Many people are attracted to the fanciful idea of a chamomile lawn. Chamomile is a herb with deliciously scented leaves, reminiscent of stewed apples – but it is by no means as hard-wearing as grass, and if you do manage to create a chamomile lawn, it is to look at only, not for sitting on. As with many herbs, the scent is released on contact, by rubbing or brushing against the leaves. The plant has a tendency to die back and is difficult to establish. And making one can be quite expensive. (You might, of course, make a small chamomile lawn within a larger lawn – but you will have to mow round it, not over it.) If anyone ever asks you to make them a chamomile lawn, try to talk them out of it.

The site must be well-drained and in full sun (growth will be patchy in shade). Ideally, choose from the non-flowering varieties, which are usually more compact than the flowering kinds. You need to buy individual plants in pots, then plant them 10–20cm apart. A chamomile lawn is not robust enough to be mown with a lawn mower but is best trimmed with scissors – a very good reason for keeping it as small as possible.

A chamomile seat would be a good compromise – though this should also be considered ornamental rather than useful, as the plants will not withstand being sat on for long periods. The idea of afternoon tea on a chamomile lawn is something of an unrealizable conceit.

*These techniques can be a valuable part of your armoury. Use them to create a range of shapes for alternative uses in other parts of the garden, perhaps to mark beds in a potager or even when laying paving and decking. (Historically, they were used for setting out carpet bedding in Victorian 'gardenesque' schemes.) For elegant scrolls (perhaps for box hedging in a knot garden), mark out two separate circles of different sizes, then run a rope or length of hosepipe around them in an S-shape. Cut out the desired length.

MOSS

If there is already plenty of moss in an existing lawn (or even in the borders), you might consider digging this up and creating a small moss lawn in a dark, shady area (exactly where you'd have problems establishing a grass lawn) – dare I say it, as part of a Japanese garden? Again, moss will not take much wear, and as the ground has to be damp to sustain good growth, it is not suitable for sitting on. But it looks nice and is a recognizably different shade of green to lawn grass.

ARTIFICIAL LAWNS

Well – why not? An artificial lawn is fun (and, dare I say it, gives an ironic touch) on a roof garden where grass cannot be reasonably expected to grow. It can also be used in other areas where a natural lawn cannot be established – for instance, in a very shady garden. It is often very difficult to tell the difference between artificial grass and the real thing.

Synthetic grass was developed initially for sports use and is often used for indoor exhibitions where a conventional grass lawn would be impractical. In a garden, it needs to be laid over compacted layers of aggregate and sand, just like paving (see Chapter 9). Because there is a firm base under it, a synthetic lawn is never so soft underfoot as a growing lawn.

Don't be fooled into thinking that it is maintenance-free. While you don't have to mow or water it, the material can become dusty and will need regular brushing and washing, just like a carpet (and, like carpet, it should be laid with the pile all lying in the same direction). You can do this with a pressure washer – if you're on that roof garden – or alternatively hose the lawn down with a strong jet of water.

You can have as big a problem with drainage as on a regular, growing lawn. Ideally, it should be laid with a very slight slope (as for hard landscaping) so surface water can run off freely – only a small volume of water will drain through it. In a wet area, moss can appear if the grass stays moist over a prolonged period. Treat this with a standard moss killer or algicide such as is used for paving.

Restoring a neglected lawn

Neglected lawns are easy to identify. There may be ragged edges, bare patches, lumps and bumps, and mossy areas. Different types of grass may have established themselves and there may also be lawn weeds – daisies, buttercups, clover and plantains.

DEALING WITH MOSS

Moss on a lawn is a sure sign of poor drainage – possibly localized, in small, heavily used patches – and this has to be addressed as a priority.

The moss represents the end result of a vicious cycle. Particular parts of a lawn (for instance, by a shed door) always see more use than others. Here, with repeated wear, the grass tends to die back, exposing the bare earth. This compacts underfoot, so water cannot drain through and

Jackie Herald

This lawn is manifestly in poor condition, showing patchy growth and areas of moss.

instead settles on the surface, inevitably attracting mosses and lichens, against which the grass cannot compete. You need to deal not only with the moss but with the drainage issue, or the problem will recur.

First, apply a moss killer. Treated moss rapidly dies and turns brown, after which you can rake it off. Fork over the bald patches and work in some grit (to improve the drainage). Loosen the upper surface and sow with grass seed.

BUMPS AND HOLLOWS

Over time, ground can subside here and there and an inherited lawn may not present a flat surface. An uneven lawn is difficult to mow – but minor bumps and dips in the surface are easily dealt with. Cut a cross over the area with a sharp knife or half-moon cutter, then peel back the quarters – a much easier job than it sounds. If you're dealing with a bump, dig out excess soil then fold the turves back over. If it's a dip, feed in a mix of good topsoil and sharp sand. In either case, keep folding over and pulling back the turf until you achieve a flat surface. Once you're satisfied, firm the turf well and water it.

OTHER PROBLEMS

Weedy lawns can be tackled with a lawn weedkiller (which miraculously can distinguish between the slim-leaved grasses and the more rounded ones of lawn plantains and convolvulus). Yellow patches on a lawn suggest a nitrogen deficiency in that area, easily dealt with by an application of a lawn feed. If the whole lawn is yellow, drought is the problem – and that's usually temporary. The grass will green up again with a good watering (or shower of rain).

Moles are trickier. Everyone knows if they've got a mole (which seem to be prevalent near water, for some reason) by the tell-tale molehills that appear on the lawn. This is no time for sentiment if you are serious about eradicating this pest – call in the services of a mole-catcher. Most other forms of deterrent are likely to make a temporary impact only.

GENERAL LAWN IMPROVEMENT

A job definitely worth doing is clearing the lawn of thatch. This is a build-up of old bits of grass and other material that collects around each blade towards the base. This material knits together (hence 'thatch'), forming an impermeable layer right on top of the soil, and guess what – it prevents water getting down to the grass roots, leading to poor growth. You can rake it off, either with an ordinary rake or a special lawn rake (which has extra-long, flexible tines, like an oversize back-scratcher). Either way – it is seriously back-breaking work.

You are then *supposed* to spike all over the lawn (with a garden fork) or special machine that makes slits in the ground – which will improve drainage. I say 'supposed' because in the process you actually compact soil around the tines as they drive through the earth. Machines that actually remove thin plugs of soil may be preferable if you know the ground is basically heavy with a high clay content. Brush over a mix of lawn sand and garden compost or earth improver. Finally, oversow with grass seed to thicken up the sward.

At the very least, lawns appreciate a feed as much as any other plant. If you are using a lawn fertilizer, look for one that contains iron (Fe). Iron does not actually benefit the growth in any measurable way – but it does darken the green, making any lawn look instantly healthier.

Wildflower meadows

A wildflower meadow comprises a mix of native annual plants grown in grass. The grass is left largely uncut and the flowering plants are allowed to grow until they disperse their seed – which will then germinate and flower the following year. This self-seeding has an easily overlooked knock-on effect. While you may start off with a mix of plants, the local conditions – soil type, typical climate and seasonal weather patterns (never the same from one year to the next) – will tend to favour particular species. In time, these will become the dominant population. After a few years, the meadow will consist of one plant only – poppies, ox-eye daisies or meadowsweet, for instance. You either have to live with this outcome, or plan to remake the meadow every few years.

Pictorial Meadows

A flowering meadow has been created to break up a large lawn.

Wildflower meadows are somewhat akin to Piet Oudolf's prairie style of planting (see Chapter 1) in that all the plants grow pretty much to the same height. While a wildflower meadow is theoretically self-maintaining, it is in no way low maintenance. It has to be *managed*. But, for the few short weeks in the year when the plants are in flower, meadows are spectacularly beautiful – and alive with insect life.

A wildflower meadow does not equate with wild gardening or even necessarily with an informal scheme. A patch of wildflowers can look sensational when used to break up a large lawn in an otherwise formal garden. If the patch is square or rectangular, you can contrive a neat conflict between formal design and the informal, 'natural' quality of the planting.

There are three important things to bear in mind before embarking on a meadow. First, you can make either a spring or summer meadow (in other words, you can't combine spring- and summer-flowering plants in the same patch of ground – the management regime militates against this). Second, the site must be in full sun (you might at a pinch get away with a spring meadow around fruit trees that are late into leaf, though the other options discussed subsequently may be more successful). Third, the soil must be of low fertility. Wildflowers are adapted to subsistence living – any soil nutrients will only benefit the grass, which will rip away, allowing the wildflowers little chance.

MAKING THE MEADOW

Seed mixes (for spring or summer) that also contain grass seed are available if you are making the meadow from scratch. In this instance, prepare the site as described previously for a lawn, but do not add any fertilizer or organic matter.

It's often best to create a meadow in an existing lawn, especially a somewhat neglected one as the grass may well have exhausted most of the nutrients in the soil. Mark out the area to be sown, then either treat it with weedkiller or strip off the turf with a spade. Removing the turf will actually benefit the wildflowers, as you are reducing the depth of topsoil and hence the nutrient content overall. Dig over the ground and rake it level before sowing. Sow a spring meadow in autumn and a summer meadow in spring.

Seed is cheap, but you cannot guarantee the results, even in the first year. For a more predictable (if more expensive) outcome, use plug plants – but only if you are creating the meadow area within an existing lawn. Simply strip off alternate squares of turf within the area (the grass in the other squares can be allowed to grow normally), then plant the plugs. Seeded

Pictorial Meadows

This planting reverses the usual – an area of lawn has been carved out of a larger meadow.

mats are available that can be rolled out and laid directly on prepared, bare earth – a quick solution, if relatively expensive.

MAINTAINING THE MEADOW

Flowering meadows are not mown in the conventional way – they need to be cut with a sickle. For a spring meadow, wait until the plants have flowered and shed their seed. Then cut to a height of around 8cm from the ground. For a neat look, cut again at three-weekly intervals or – if you don't have time for this – again in late summer. Either way, it's important to gather up and dispose of the clippings. Left in place, they will rot down and boost the soil fertility. A summer meadow does not need cutting in the first year. Assuming you sow or plant in spring, the plants should flower the same year. In the year following (and in subsequent years), make a cut in spring to around 8cm from ground level. One to three further cuts may be needed but make the last one no later than late spring, after which all (including the flowering plants) can be left to develop unchecked.

To cut, grasp a handful of the topgrowth in one hand, then swing the sickle through it at the appropriate height. By all means wear medieval costume when using the sickle; the important thing is that the blade is sharp and that your cutting motion is away from your body – for obvious reasons.

SIMPLER ALTERNATIVES

To create the look of a meadow (though without any coloured flowers), leave an area of the lawn unmown and just allow the grass to grow and flower (not good for hayfever sufferers and asthmatics, however).* You can even cut the grass within the area to different lengths. This can look sensational in an otherwise formal scheme. A patch of unmown grass is supposed to benefit wildlife too. Frogs, toads and grass snakes and a range of invertebrates may well shelter in the long grass in summer, but larks and other ground-breeding birds are unlikely to nest in it – they need much more space and prefer open fields.

If you must have flowers, you can create the look of a meadow with spring bulbs. These also offer the best option if you want flowers around deciduous trees. For summer flowers – at a pinch – you can try establishing certain robust perennials in an open part of a lawn. Peonies, achilleas, echinops, daylilies (*Hemerocallis*) and many late-flowering daisies are robust enough to compete with grass (though growth will not be as lush as in conventional beds and borders). If you are not too much of a purist, you might also consider adding tough roses such as *Rosa rugosa* and modern ground-cover types.

Any of these present the designer with a low-maintenance, longer-term alternative to a more conventional meadow.

*In a rural area, you may find an influx of cow parsley and, less desirably, docks and nettles (though the last are good for butterflies).

WATER (AND ROCK GARDENS)

Historically, water has usually been introduced into gardens to cool the air – generally in hot climates. Before you begin planning a water feature (dreadful term, but there is no other), ask yourself whether its presence is really necessary.

Water features became popular largely because of their consistent use in TV makeover programmes. I understand the logic of this. The effect of a water feature (generally involving moving water) is instant, and you do not have to wait for plants to grow. An unfortunate effect of this is that nowadays water is often considered an essential element, a 'must-have' in a design. If you are doing this professionally, you may have no choice in the matter, if this is what a client wants. However, you might point out that, leaving swimming pools and jacuzzis out of it, a water feature is never a cheap option.

Never install a pond of any kind if you or your client have small children (in fact, you are quite likely to have to fill in an existing pond in that scenario). Water draws everyone to it like a magnet. Even grown-ups have been known to fall in.

Ecologists are particularly fond of water in a garden as a garden pool will attract all manner of wildlife that does indeed add an extra element and can be an important habitat. Water snails do not greatly contribute to the scene – but mayflies, frogs and toads definitely do. The received wisdom is that these are beneficial, as they eat garden pests (I have never actually observed a frog devouring a slug, but it's believed that they do). Many visiting insects pollinate plants – important if you have a fruit garden nearby, but not otherwise likely to be critical. An area of the garden swarming with insects can be a delight – or not, as these can multiply to become plagues in summer. And not everyone wants frogs wandering into the kitchen. Actually, I wonder to what extent the 'benefits' can be quantified. In excavating the site, you are actually removing a large volume of organic material that is home to wildlife – but mainly invertebrate, these are often microscopic. Slugs, centipedes and nematodes – even bacteria – have as much right to exist as bees and butterflies. A truly ecological approach would see the spoil from digging utilized elsewhere on site (see 'Rock gardens', on p. 122).

That said – water can be a magical element in any garden.

Still water features

At the risk of stating the obvious, water always finds its own level. In fact, in design terms, this is its strength, as water presents a surface that is guaranteed to be perfectly flat. It is already leading towards formality and always works well in a scheme devised around strict proportions and strong verticals. In an informal setting, it inevitably provides contrast. A still pool works best on a site that is already level – and may draw attention to any slight slope in the ground (especially if you are planning a formal pool near the house). Some skill or guile on your part

Jackie Herald/Cleve West

Here, the stones set in the gravel path are allowed to run into shallow water – a visually unifying device.

Jackie Herald/Cleve West

A larger view of the previous. In this formal layout, the water is left unplanted.

may be needed to disguise this. A pool can be regularly shaped (circular, oval, square or oblong – which suits a formal scheme) or be irregular – a rough kidney shape being the usual choice. There's no need to be hide-bound by this, but a formal pool usually works well near the house, perhaps incorporated in a patio and reflecting – literally – some of the proportions to be found on the house. An informal pool suits a more relaxed area of the site.

A familiar mantra is that an informal pool is going to be planted – presumably on the basis that its random shape is not likely to be a strong element of the design. Thick planting will also blur its outline, making it less clearly defined. Formal pools are often unplanted or may contain only a few plants. The emphasis should be on the proportions and the sheer beauty of an unbroken, mirror-like stretch of water, and planting can distract from this. Neither is – or need be – strictly adhered to.

WILDLIFE/INFORMAL POOL

A pool that is going to be used to grow water plants and attract wildlife must be in full sun. The reasons are strictly practical. Most water plants need sun to grow and flower well. In shade, water rapidly becomes murky and green through algal and lichen growth (actually – this is *always* a potential problem, wherever the pool is, but less so in sun). Water plants are rampant growers (why wouldn't they be, given a constant supply of moisture at their feet?) and in shade will make masses of leafy growth with precious few flowers.

The usual advice is that the pool should be well away from overhanging deciduous trees, but I think this should be taken with a pinch of salt. It's true that a tree will shed its leaves (and flowers, if it produces any) in the water, where they will rot and potentially cause a horrible smell, to say nothing of creating an environment that may be toxic to plants and wildlife. But it is virtually impossible to keep fallen leaves out of the water in autumn anyway – they will blow in from other parts of the garden and any neighbouring gardens. Dealing with them just becomes part of the annual maintenance. Besides, many trees look sensational next to water (even with stems trailing in the water, if it's a weeping willow) and this can be a strong element of the design – the inevitable tension between vertical and horizontal. In nature, the margins of any stretch of water are often home to moisture-loving trees such as dogwoods or willows. And never underestimate the impact of a naked deciduous tree reflected in still water in winter. If you can manage it, contrive a subtle union between the volumes and proportions of tree and water.

A more important piece of advice concerns the size of the pool and this to some extent relies on your knowledge of the second law of thermodynamics. A body of water heats up in the sun (and there's some water loss from the surface through evaporation) then cools. To avoid too steep a fluctuation of temperature in the body of water itself (which will have an adverse effect on plants and wildlife), the surface area should be at least $10m^2$ with a depth of at least 45cm (at its deepest). Small, shallow pools heat up rapidly in hot weather and there's generally a contingent surge in green algal growth that will choke out other plants. The depth of 45cm not only helps keep the temperature down, as water in the lower portion will stay cool, but allows you to grow water lilies (*Nymphaea*) – as you must. Because the sting in the tail is that, to moderate the temperature in summer, two-thirds to three-quarters of the water surface should be covered – to shelter frogs (which will go for a dip to cool off on hot days) and other aquatic wildlife, as well as to prevent the water from overheating. The floating leaves of water lilies do the job perfectly.

Once established, however, the water in a pool is self-regulating and does not need to be replaced. Ever.

It follows that if you are working on a garden that already has a (probably neglected) pond that is a lurid pea green swamp, one of your first actions may well be to get rid of it – or possibly make it bigger. In all likelihood, it is either too small or too shallow.

FORMAL POOL

A formal pool, strictly geometric, has always been an integral centrepiece of an Islamic garden (as described in Chapter 1). Formal pools can be raised – in other words, the surface of the water can be above ground level – or sunk in the ground so the water is flush with the ground. At its most extreme, a formal pool may contain no plants at all but simply be intended as a still, reflective horizontal surface. If the intention is to keep fish in the pool, some oxygenating plants will be required as well as some soil at the base in which the fish can overwinter.

If there are to be no fish or plants – just water – this won't be self-regulating in the way that a wildlife pool is. You will need to keep the water clear with a chemical agent. In this case, the base

Jackie Herald/Luciano Giubbilei

The water here is too shallow for planting – it is left clear to contrast with the lush planting to either side.

of the pool is always visible and can be concealed or decorated with pebbles, tiles or even glass beads. If there are to be fish in the pool, add a biological filter – this will keep the water pure but not clear. For clear water, add an ultraviolet clarifier. (Filters are sometimes housed outside the water and the water is pumped through them – in which case, they have to be concealed, most easily with planting – and connection to a power source is necessary.) All these filters will need regular cleaning to keep them working efficiently.

A formal pool can incorporate a fountain – to devastating effect. It's also possible to light pools, not from above but with lights actually in the water (and they can be coloured). You can see why designers are often attracted to the use of water in a garden – once installed, the effect is instantly gratifying.

For reasons that will become clear when we discuss construction, I caution against formal pools. Not only must the angles be exact – if the pool is square or rectangular – but, if visible from the house, the edges must line up with it perfectly if they are not to be an eyesore (see Chapter 10 for methods of plotting straight lines).*

RAISED POOLS

A raised pool (with the water level higher than the ground level – the base of the pool may or may not also be sunk into the ground to some extent) presents certain problems of engineering in construction that are way beyond the expertise of most designers. Leaving aside the geometric precision with which they have to be placed and built, there is the issue of weight. A large volume of water is heavy, and the walls of the pool have to be sturdy enough to withstand the outwards pressure. Furthermore, a body of water above ground level is much more likely to freeze in winter than one below (which is insulated to some extent by the soil around it). The expansion of the ice puts further pressure on the pool walls, which may buckle or even crack.** The water temperature will also climb more steeply in summer than in a pool that's sunk in the ground, increasing the stress on any fish – and indeed wildlife and plants.

However, a raised pool, if it is possible to make one, does offer certain possibilities. The walls of the pool, since they have to be fairly thick, can incorporate seating or planting, in the manner of a raised bed.

*Very experienced professional designers often subvert expectations by creating quadrilateral pools with unequal sides and acute and obtuse angles, perhaps to create a false perspective or to harmonize or be in tension with some other element in the garden.

**An interesting example is at York Gate, Adel (the garden of the Gardeners Royal Benevolent Society), where what presents as a very elegant narrow oblong raised tank of water is in fact two separate tanks bounded by a single wall. It was found during construction that the wall could not sustain the weight of the water unless it was divided.

OASE (UK) Ltd

This gentle stream is designed – and planted – to look natural.

A watercourse is a series of linked pools. Take care that all the water is caught in each successive pool.

Moving water features

Whether they incorporate fountains or not, the preceding types of water feature all fundamentally present a still, mirror-like surface. Water that's kept moving – whether it's a gentle, meandering trickle or a thundering torrent – is always changing. I am somewhat ambivalent towards moving water in a garden (unless it's a natural stream). The constant sound of running water can be an irritant, not only to you (or the owners of the garden) but to the neighbours. It's on a par with wind chimes, bonfires and barbecues. It is not a particularly restful presence.

A moving water feature can be natural-looking or a more sculptural piece of deliberate artifice in a more formal context. It may indeed even include sculpture. But while the goddess Hebe might logically pour youth-enhancing water from an urn, lions and dragons spewing water from their mouths create a more unreal impression. With an eye on proportion and volumes, you may prefer abstraction. (Beware though – great slabs of polished granite with water washing down them can give a garden a corporate air, and even less happily put you in mind of a men's public lavatory.) Watercourses – where water cascades down a series of linked pools – can be formal or informal.*

*A striking recent example of a formal watercourse is to be seen at Alnwick Castle, though you will in all probability be working on much more modest schemes.

114

OASE (UK) Ltd

This watercourse, conceived as a series of steps or shelves, is manifestly artificial. Note the extent of the pool, necessary to supply the required volume of water.

OASE (UK) Ltd

With its quantity of large rocks and impressive volume of water, this thunderous waterfall would be expensive to install.

Whatever the design, a pump to lift the water has to be installed in a reservoir. (In the case of a watercourse, the reservoir is the lowest pool, but it can also be concealed below ground. You will need to be able to access the reservoir for maintenance, however.) The reservoir has to hold a sufficient volume of water to maintain an uninterrupted flow, while the pump has to be powerful enough to lift it to the required height. If your brain is starting to hurt, relax – suppliers of the necessary equipment will do the calculations for you and tell you exactly which pump you need and how big the reservoir should be. All you need to know is the height you want to lift the water and the distance it is required to travel. And when you are planning, remember that the pipe that carries the water from the pump in the reservoir to the source will have to be cunningly concealed. You may be surprised at quite how large the reservoir has to be; when all the water is running through the system, it still has to appear to be relatively full. If the reservoir is to be a large pool, I'm afraid you'll have to forget water lilies if the water is to be constantly in motion. They will grow only in still water. So, for a cascade into a lily pond, the pump has to be idle for most of the time.

Moving water features (with no plants) can be made successfully in shade. A gargoyle, lion's head or mask can spill water into a stone basin to cool the air in summer. While you'll still want to keep the water clear, any mosses and lichens that appear will only add to its charm.

Making a pool

Make no mistake about it – digging a pond is hard work. You also have to dispose of the spoil, either by incorporating it elsewhere in the garden or hiring a skip. If you are making an informal watercourse, you can use it for bedding in rocks (see also 'Rock gardens', on p. 122).

For an informal pool (usually kidney-shaped), use a flexible liner (sold either on the roll or as pre-cut squares or oblongs). The liner should be laid in one piece. It's theoretically possible to join sections of liner, rather as you would repair a puncture in a bicycle tyre, but it's better to avoid this. Any seal has to be watertight and emptying a filled pool to repair a future split will be a pain. The material usually has a guarantee of ten years, but in practice is usually much longer lived. Use butyl to line a round, oval or kidney-shaped pond. It is less suitable for shapes with squares and rectangles (or triangles, come to that), as the material forms unsightly pleats at the corners. It is also easiest if the pool is to have gently sloping sides, though it is possible, even desirable, to incorporate a shelf for marginal plants (see 'Stocking the pool' on p. 119). The material also has the beauty that it can be cut to shape.

For any shape with corners, use a pre-cast rigid liner (making sure, of course, that you can easily get it on site). Pre-cast liners can also offer the simplest option for a raised pool. For a reservoir that will be below ground or otherwise hidden, you could use a water tank from a builders' merchant. Informal shapes are also available pre-cast, but are trickier to install than a flexible liner – plus, you may not be able to find one of the exact dimensions you require. They normally have a shelf around the perimeter for planting. Whichever type of liner you opt for, preparation is the same.

USING A FLEXIBLE LINER

Mark out the shape of the pool with a length of rope or hosepipe, held in position (if necessary) with short stakes driven into the ground to either side. This is a good opportunity to establish that the pool is actually in the best position visually and that the size is appropriate. It's easy to make any adjustments at this stage – later on, it won't be so simple. Check that the chosen site is level by laying a plank with a spirit level across the area in both directions. If one side is notice-ably higher, part of the liner will be visible when the pond is filled with water. Not only is this unsightly, but exposure to hot sun on that side may crack the liner and shorten its life.

Cut along the line indicated by the hose or rope with a spade or half-moon cutter. If you're digging the pond in a lawn, strip off the turf – this makes excellent composting material or you can use it to line the planting hole of a large tree or shrub. Start to dig out the ground to the required depth. If you're not going to skip all the spoil, keep the topsoil and subsoil in separate piles. You *may* be able to dispose of the topsoil around the garden (though I don't entirely approve of this), but you certainly shouldn't do it with the subsoil, which, if it cannot be put to legitimate good use elsewhere, should be dumped in the skip.

If the pond is to be planted, excavate to a depth of 10–15cm around the perimeter to create a shelf for marginal plants (planted in special aquatic mesh pots with the whole of the lower part of the plant submerged). It's worth taking the trouble to make the shelf level at this stage, otherwise the plants won't stand upright. You can also incorporate a 'beach' to one side. Rather than creating a shelf, make a gentle slope. This is supposed to provide an escape route for any small mammals that fall into the pond – though I have never encountered any that are stupid enough to do this (unless they do it at night). More likely, the beach will be used by birds for bathing in summer.

Dig out the base of the pond to a depth of around 45cm or more. If you are using a flexible liner, it's less critical that the bottom of the pond is strictly level, but it is important to remove any large stones – the weight of the water will press the liner against them, possibly causing tears. Tread over the excavated area to consolidate the soil. Check the level of the pond at the perimeter and carry out any further excavation as necessary. Once you've dug the hole, it can be advisable to delay the next stage and continue the following day. This allows you to check that you have not dug beneath the water table – in which case the lower part of the pond will have filled with water. Should this be the case, the best option is to rethink this aspect of the project.*

Line the base of the pond, either with a special fleece or building sand (or even lengths of old carpet or newspaper). Unroll the liner, then spread it over the excavated area. Lay it loosely and make sure that any creases around the edge (there are bound to be some) are evenly distributed. Spread some of the excavated topsoil on the base, to a depth of around 8cm. Start to fill with water. Don't worry about the soil turning to mud initially – a newly filled pond always looks very murky with the particles of soil floating around in it, but these soon sink to the base, leaving the water clear. The weight of the water actually stretches the liner slightly, pushing it into the excavated hole. As the level rises, even up any pleats that appear around the edge. Fill right to the top.

Leave it to settle for a day or so, topping up as necessary. Then you can trim back any excess liner from around the edge. Now comes the rub. You have to disguise the edge of the liner. If the pond is in a lawn, it would be nice to be able to turf right to the edge – but this isn't generally practical, as it leads to problems with mowing. Some kind of paving around part of the perimeter is desirable, if only because it makes maintenance easier (particularly if you have to fish an electric pump out periodically). But slabs laid all around the edge tend to accentuate the fact that the pond is artificial. This is one area where decking suddenly presents an obvious solution (see Chapter 9). If you incorporated a slope, lay shingle or pebbles over this section. Marginal plants can help soften the rest of the perimeter (see 'Stocking the pool' on p. 119).

The water in a pool rapidly matures to become a self-sufficient eco-system. If you want to speed things up even more, introduce a bucketful of water from an established pond nearby.

*Don't assume that the weight of the water within the liner will hold it down. The water table as it rises will lift the liner, causing the water within it to spill out to either side. The water level will drop once the water table falls back.

PRE-FORMED LINERS

A pre-formed liner is more problematic, as your excavations have to be very precise if you are going to avoid any subsidence once it is filled with water. Most pre-formed liners are moulded with a marginal shelf (though the following applies also to formally shaped types that are not intended for plants).

Set the liner in position and check the level carefully. Mark the outline on the ground with a series of vertical canes driven in around the perimeter about 45cm apart. Run a rope or hosepipe around these to mark the shape. Following this line, dig down to the depth of the marginal shelf. Then set the liner in position and press down hard to leave an imprint on the ground of the liner's base. Remove the liner, then dig out the base to the depth of the liner plus an additional 5cm. That extra depth allows for a foundation.

Spade in a layer of sand, level it, and place the liner in position. Now is the time for any adjustments to the level. Check the marginal shelf carefully for any dips and hollows (you can fill in slight dips with sand). Start to fill with water. Check the level at intervals – if the base is not perfectly flat, the pond will tilt slightly as it gains weight. You can lift it out and make any adjustments reasonably easily at this stage – less so if you wait until the liner is full before checking.

STOCKING THE POOL

If the pool is to be a habitat for wildlife, you will need a good range of plants. As previously stated, water plants are extremely vigorous, so growing them in containers is virtually essential if their aggressive tendencies are to be held in check.

Deep-water plants

With leaves that float on the water surface, these plants are essential for maintaining an even temperature during hot weather in summer. Waterlilies (*Nymphaea*) are the obvious choice. There are hundreds of varieties of varying degrees of vigour. Choose an appropriate variety for the size of pool. Miniatures are suitable for small pools. As an alternative, *Orontium aquaticum* is neat-growing with intriguing flowers that look like smouldering cigarettes. It's a little unorthodox, but it is worth trying one of the hardier arum lilies (*Zantedeschia aethiopica*) as an aquatic, allowing its glassy green arrow-like leaves and clear white spathes to rise Excalibur-like above the water.

Marginal water plants

These are plants that appreciate permanently wet soil – some even tolerate having the lower part of their stems in water as well. Grow them in conventional pots or aquatic baskets that are stood on the shelves around the perimeter of the pool. It may be necessary to raise the pots on bricks to achieve the desired level (this is when you'll be glad you checked the levels when you dug the pond). Note that many of these plants are also suitable for growing in borders where the soil does not dry out.

Bog plants
These plants like damp soil around their roots but prefer their crowns (the point where the roots meet the topgrowth) above the water level. Use deep pots or stand them on bricks.

Oxygenating plants
Essential for maintaining water clarity and for sheltering invertebrates and fish (if there are any), these plants float just below the water surface. Without being intrinsically beautiful in their own right, they absorb excess mineral salts and starve out algae as well as giving out oxygen.

Surface floaters
Plants whose leaves float on the surface while their roots trail in the water below (unlike deep-water plants, the roots do not anchor the plants in the bed of the pond) are not essential but can make an interesting addition to a pool. The water soldier (*Stratiotes aloides*) sinks to the bottom of the pool in autumn to overwinter in the mud, then rises to the surface in spring to thrust a rosette of spiky leaves above water level.

OXYGENATING PLANTS	COMMON NAME
Callitriche hermaphroditica	Water starwort
Callitriche palustris	Common waterwort
Ceratophyllum demersum	Hornwort
Fontinalis antipyretica	Water moss
Hottonia palustris	Water violet
Hydrocharis morsus-ranae	Frogbit
Lagarosiphon major	Curly waterweed
Potamogeton crispus	Curled pondweed
Ranunculus aquaticus	Water buttercup

Plants suitable for growing as marginals

BOTANICAL NAME	COMMON NAME
Butomus umbellatus.	Flowering rush
Calla palustris	Water arum
Caltha palustris	Marsh marigold
Houttuynia cordata	Chameleon plant
Ligularia	
Lobelia cardinalis.	Cardinal flower
Lysichiton	Skunk cabbage
Myosotis scorpioides	Water forget-me-not
Pontederia cordata	Pickerel weed

BOG GARDENS

One of the best solutions to dealing with an area of wet ground is to create a bog garden – filled with plants that appreciate permanently damp soil. Natural ponds are often bordered by areas of wet ground. Unfortunately, this does not hold true for artificial ponds. If dug in dry ground, the soil surrounding them remains resolutely dry. This causes a problem for any designer who wishes his or her pool to look as natural as possible – the plants you may feel will make the ideal contribution to the scene simply will not thrive.

General soil improvement – digging in quantities of organic matter – can help (see Chapter 2). A more permanent solution is to create an artificial boggy area to one side of the pool, using a butyl liner such as is used in making an informal pond, as described previously. Excavate an area of soil to a depth of around 45cm. Level the base, then top with a layer of building sand. (You can also dig deeper at one end to allow for deep-rooted bog plants such as *Gunnera*.) Stretch a sheet of liner over the sand, then puncture this all over with a garden fork or sharp knife – you are aiming to slow down drainage, not prevent it. Fill with garden soil, then plant up as required.

Unlike naturally boggy soil, there is no ground water that keeps an artificial bog garden permanently moist. In periods of drought, it may be necessary to water this area of the garden to maintain good growth. Even with this proviso, I am dubious about artificial bog gardens – the soil both above and beneath the liner is likely to turn sour in time and the surface may develop a crust of algae and moulds.

To grow isolated, moisture-loving plants next to an artificial pond (such as the gunnera mentioned previously, which is too large for use as a marginal in most situations) sink a large container – or bucket with holes drilled in the base – into the ground. Water as required to maintain the appropriate degree of wetness.

WATERCOURSES

If the watercourse is to comprise a series of linked pools, it is easiest to use a flexible liner for each, as you can then create a lip over which the water will pour into the next pool. For a gentle stream, use a length of liner – you can conceal the liner with pebbles and rocks.

You can see the budget rising. But, as expensive as large rocks are, the money is swallowed up less by the materials than by the manpower. Creating a watercourse is ultimately a matter of trial and error, especially if the water is to cascade over rocks, which have to be moved into position then adjusted. It's critical that the maximum amount of water in the system finds its way back to the reservoir. Some will inevitably be lost on its progress through evaporation, but splashes that land outside the liner or the next pool will soon deplete the amount available. It can take several hours, even a couple of days, to get this right.

Rock gardens

This is parenthesized in the title to this chapter – because rock gardens (or rockeries) have gone completely out of fashion. I can hardly call to mind a single one I have seen in recent years. Nevertheless, a rock garden, or some other kind of raised feature, allows you to deal with the spoil from all your excavations – and you may well be using rocks in making a watercourse, as described above.

From the planting point of view, rock gardens are eminently suitable for growing alpines (plants from mountainous regions, not just the Alps) – small, low-growing, usually tuft-forming, hardy perennials (such as androsace, dianthus and phlox). These have a low nutrient requirement (so need little soil), are usually tolerant of drought and freezing temperatures, but must have swift drainage. Most need full sun. For a rock garden in shade, concentrate instead on small ferns, hostas and mosses.

A rock garden usually offers a very successful solution to a steeply sloping part of a garden. If it's on a big scale, plant it with big plants – trailing or creeping shrubs such as winter jasmine (*Jasminum nudiflorum*), *Ceanothus thyrsiflorus* var. *repens* and *Cotoneaster horizontalis*. These will produce as effective a cascade as can ever be achieved with water.

BUILDING THE ROCKERY

Dig over the site and remove all traces of weeds. Mound up the soil (unless you are already working on sloping ground). If you are using excavated soil, make the mound with the subsoil. Set the rocks into the soil, larger ones towards the base, burying each one by between a third to a half. Tilt the rocks slightly so that any rainwater runs off or back into the soil – definitely not onto the plants (equally, water should not drip from one rock onto plants below).

Arrange the chosen plants in the gaps among the stones, adjusting the angles of the stones as necessary.

PLANTS FOR SUNNY ROCKERIES	COMMON NAME
Aubrieta	
Campanula portenschlagiana	Adria bellflower
Dianthus (small types)	Carnation, pink
Erigeron karvinskianus	Mexican fleabane
Euphorbia myrsinites	Broad-leaved glaucous spurge
Geranium (small types)	
Gypsophila repens	Creeping gypsophila
Lewisia	
Sedum (small types)	Stonecrop
Sempervivum	House leek
Thymus	Thyme

PLANTS FOR SHADY ROCKERIES*	COMMON NAME
Asarina procumbens	Trailing snapdragon
Cardamine trifolia	Trifoliate bittercress
Daphne blagayana	Balkan daphne
Ferns (dwarf species)	
Gaultheria procumbens	Checkerberry
Heuchera	Coral flower
Hepatica nobilis	Hepatica
Hosta (dwarf cultivars)	
Primula (some)	
Prunella grandiflora	Self-heal
Saxifraga stolonifera	Strawberry saxifrage
Saxifraga x urbium	London pride
Tiarella cordifolia	Foam flower

*Many dwarf conifers and rhododendrons are also shade-tolerant. In a large rockery, Japanese maples (forms of *Acer japonicum* and *Acer palmatum*) can also be added.

8

WALLS, FENCES AND HEDGES

Walls, fences and hedges set the boundaries not only around a garden but within it, to delineate separate areas. In a large space, they can create individual 'rooms' – à la Hidcote or Sissinghurst – that allow for seasonal planting and define proportions within the space. You can also use low walls, fences and hedges to divide up the space while retaining a general view over the whole of it. You may also need some form of screening to conceal a utility area – where the bins, compost and water butt are kept or where the washing is hung out to dry, for instance.

While it's easy to think of walls, fences and hedges solely in terms of utility – creating security and privacy – aesthetics need never (in fact should never) be overlooked. Not only are these barriers often permanently in view, but they have an important role as the backdrop to everything within the garden. They need to integrate into the design – otherwise it can be all too obvious that they are concealing some eyesore and, in a sense, even draw attention to it, which rather defeats the purpose. Always take into account the shade that they will cast – and, in the case of hedges, the moisture that the plants will drink up from the neighbouring soil. This will have an impact on plant growth nearby – including that of grass.

Note that solid walls and fences (and dense hedges) do not do a particularly effective job of sheltering a garden from strong wind – in fact, they can create turbulence. To reduce the impact of wind, a fence that incorporates some trellis or a deciduous hedge can make a more effective windbreak. Relatively speaking, a hedge needs much more maintenance than a fence (which needs no more than a yearly varnish). Walls, unless painted, generally need no regular attention at all.

Walls

It's extremely unlikely that you'll ever find yourself in the position of having to build – or needing to have built – a new garden wall. The expense is often prohibitive, not just as regards materials but manpower. While Winston Churchill famously found building walls a therapeutic escape from politics, bricklaying on the whole is not a job for an amateur, and qualified bricklayers earn their money. So it's also unlikely that you would actually have to demolish a wall, unless it is unsound. Should this be necessary, consider whether it is possible, or appropriate, to re-use the bricks elsewhere in the garden – particularly if you are interested in 'sustainable' gardening and would prefer to avoid the cost of a skip. At the very least, they can be used as hardcore to support paving or to enclose a compost heap.

If you do need to build a wall, look for bricks that match those on the house (assuming it's brick-built) if it's important that house and garden integrate. If it's an older house, you may be able to source bricks of similar age and provenance from a local reclamation yard. In case this is not possible, or if old bricks are prohibitively expensive, consider using new bricks then rendering them. The render can then be painted a more sympathetic colour, either to match the house or some other area of hard landscaping in the garden. Rendering can also be used on cheaper materials such as breeze blocks.* To lighten a shady courtyard, paint walls white, or another pale colour.

While it's tempting to use walls as a support for climbers or wall shrubs – especially if they have a favourable aspect – it can sometimes be just as effective to leave a wall unadorned. If it's a stone wall or mellow, weathered old brick – a thing of beauty or interest in its own right – why not allow it to speak as it is or incorporate it into the design? A smooth expanse of unadorned concrete sweeping up to an old stone wall makes a point without the need for distracting planting.

If you are going to use low walls in a scheme, consider incorporating seating or planting into the design.

*Inspired by Yves Saint-Laurent's garden in Marrakech, Morocco, there was a vogue towards the end of the twentieth century for rendered walls (which look like traditional adobe) painted vibrant colours – in this case a rich deep saturated blue. Such colours work very well in a climate where sun is often strong – dark colours seem to soak in and absorb the light – but are much less successful in damper climates, where subtle earth tones are more appropriate.

FENCES

To most gardeners, a fence merely marks the boundaries of a garden, or perhaps surrounds the composting area or shed. But a visit to any builders' merchant or garden centre will reveal that there is a wealth of options, and your choice should be considered.

Fences are nearly always made of timber, either softwood or hardwood. Softwood comes from conifers (usually larch) and is cheap. Hardwood alternatives – such as oak or even teak – are considerably more expensive. As usual, you get what you pay for. A cheap larch lap fence

In this small garden, fencing comprising horizontal slats 'stretches' the space. A mirror enhances the effect.

Jackie Herald

The clear uprights of the bamboo canes conflict deliberately with the horizontals of the fence, creating a sense of tension.

has a maximum life of ten years (and may lose what good looks it has well within that period), whereas a hardwood equivalent will be much more durable. But no timber fencing should ever be viewed as permanent. While most timber fencing will have been pressure-treated during its manufacture to repel water, it will still need annual maintenance – a coating of wood preservative applied during still, dry weather – in the same way as other timber in the garden.

Cheap fencing has its place in a design, particularly if you are on a tight budget. Since fence panels come in standard sizes (usually 2m long, but in a range of heights), panels can always be replaced with a more expensive alternative at a later date. You may well install a cheap fence next to a new hedge to create a boundary while you are waiting for the hedge to establish – with a view to removing the fence within a few years once the plants have thickened. Wooden panels can be painted or stained (stained only darker, however), so don't feel restricted by the rather vibrant orange of the new timber. This may be necessary not only to mitigate the harsh colour of the new material, but to integrate it with other wood (including older fencing) that may already be part of the scheme. In a short time, most timber weathers down to a nondescript grey.

Jackie Herald

A high fence is needed here to create privacy – but the problem has been tackled head on. The vertical planks positively accentuate the uprights seen in the balustrade and enhance the feeling of enclosure.

Boundary fencing can have an unexpected impact on the design. Cheap larch lap panels, with the timbers running horizontally, can make a garden look longer where they are used to run at right angles to the house – to be borne in mind if you are working on a long, narrow rectangle as is typical of many town houses (you may unwittingly be exaggerating a negative aspect of the space). Conversely, they may appear to 'stretch' the far end boundary that is parallel with the house. Types with vertical timbers work well in a situation where you want to emphasize upright lines – say if you are planning a stand of birches or planting bamboo just in front of the fence. Beware of unintended clashes of verticals and horizontals, especially in a small space – or meet them head on and exploit them boldly.

If the fence – which may already be present and of sound quality – does not work for the concept you have for the garden, it can be covered with some flexible material, made from shoots of (usually) bamboo or willow wired together, sold by length on a roll. Since bamboo is mainly a plant of South and East Asia, this type can be particularly useful if you are developing an oriental look in a small garden – where there may not be room to grow living bamboo, which is particularly invasive. Willow screening can provide a rural touch in a city garden. Simply from the design point of view, these coverings can also be used to emphasize a vertical.

Jackie Herald

Upright canes lashed to the fence to the rear of this plot have been used to distract attention from the overgrown conifer beyond. Note the mowing strip at the edge of the curved lawn.

SCREENING

Some fencing has no aesthetic aspect at all and is usually used merely for practical reasons. Screening is usually sold as a tough synthetic mesh (generally green or brown) that can be stretched between uprights (the same that would be used to support fence panels). This type of screening is usually used around a kitchen garden as a barrier against deer. Being permeable, it filters wind without cutting out too much light and rainfall. Screening can be used on roof gardens, where it not only filters winds but actually gives the space the air of being a garden – as well as creating privacy from prying eyes from neighbouring roof gardens. It can also be used to screen an ugly view without taking up valuable ground space.

In an exposed situation (cold and windy), screening can be used in the short term to shelter a newly planted conifer hedge on the windward side. Many conifers are tough and hardy only once established – as young plants they are vulnerable to cold. Leave the screen in position for the first two to three years after planting. Allow a gap of up to 45cm between the screen and the plants to allow for growth.

TRELLIS

Trellis panels have their uses, and not only as a potential support for plants. If you are dealing with a potentially large stretch of (possibly) featureless fencing, you can break this up by using lower panels here and there and topping them with a length of trellis. Within the garden, trellis panels on their own can be used to screen off one area from another and can support climbers that die back in winter, such as many clematis and golden hop (*Humulus lupulus* 'Aureus'), or annuals such as morning glories (*Ipomoea*), sweet peas (*Lathyrus odoratus*) or black-eyed Susan (*Thunbergia alata*) – even beans if the trellis defines a vegetable garden. The screening is effectively solid in summer, because the trellis is covered by vegetation, but more open in winter – giving glimpses of what's beyond. If this is your intention, check the aspect carefully. If you are covering the trellis with flowering climbers, the flowers will all be produced on the sunny side. Be careful also not to select too vigorous a climber – which may well pull the trellis down.* But this solution can greatly add to the dynamics of a garden, creating and separating intimate spaces in summer but opening up a larger vista in winter.

If you are growing climbers against a trellis, do not expect the stems of the plants to find their own way – they will have to be tied in just as they would to wires stretched against a solid fence or wall.

CONCRETE

Concrete screens – comprising stacked blocks of pierced concrete – are redolent of 1970s suburbia, but they deserve a revival. Their value lies in their versatility. Ideal for partition walls within a garden, they are cheap and easy to use, needing only a shallow concrete footing of around 25cm. They are held in position by upright pillars, themselves supported with reinforcing rods driven into the footing while the concrete is still wet. Reclaimed blocks are widely available.

Concrete screens do a very effective job of filtering wind and will also cast a dappled shade – unlike solid walls and fences. The blocks are also easy to lay in a curve, which extends the design possibilities. Individual blocks are sometimes used to break up an expanse of wall or can be laid in a row to raise the height of a wall.

LOW FENCES

Low fences – to a height within 1m – do no more than mark boundaries or delineate areas within a garden, but can make a significant contribution to a design.

Picket fences (comprising wooden uprights wired together) work well in a rural garden that borders open fields – assuming security is not an issue. A low fence that comprises rope swagged

---

*Hence weighty evergreens or plants with a permanent framework such as honeysuckles (*Lonicera*) are best avoided.

Rope swags work well with decking and water. Note the non-slip mesh stretched over the gangway.

OASE (UK) Ltd

between short uprights gives a nautical feel to a garden and suits decking (but please – near water only, if not the actual ocean).

A low post-and-rail fence – suitable for marking off a front lawn next to a driveway – looks very New England (think *Desperate Housewives*). For some reason, they are nearly always white and often made of a synthetic material, which will be more durable than wood. In fact, there is no simpler way to make an otherwise blank front garden look smart with the minimum effort. In conjunction with a deck, post-and-rail fencing always has a colonial look – perhaps this is something that could be exploited with the addition of banana palms or bougainvilleas in pots, plants that would logically be used in a hot climate.

Hedges

Hedges offer a relatively cheap, usually long-term alternative to a wall or fence with the downside that the barrier is not instant – the plants have to be allowed time to grow.

Additionally, a hedge needs regular maintenance. Formal hedges will have to be cut twice a year just to restrict growth and maintain clean lines. For a very smart finish, two or more further cuts will be required. Even informal hedges need regular cutting to keep them within bounds. Nevertheless, nothing gives a garden the air of being well-maintained so much as a recently cut hedge and mown lawn – and an established hedge, cut regularly for dense growth, will be as sturdy as any wall. As with trees and shrubs, hedging suddenly assumes prominence in winter, when you will appreciate its shape and the proportions of the volumes and voids.

There are many variables to consider when choosing hedging plants – think about what you are looking to achieve with the hedge and how it will integrate with the rest of the planting and the garden at large:

- Height – tall, medium, low?
- Function – boundary, windbreak screening, to provide security or privacy?
- Formal vs informal?
- Flowering/fruiting?
- Evergreen vs deciduous?
- Plain or mixed hedge?
- Habitat for wildlife?

At one extreme is the utility hedge – of small aesthetic value but necessary to block out an ugly view, shelter a garden from wind or traffic noise or, if thorny, act as a barbarous defence against potential intruders. If there's to be significant planting in front of it – such as a stand of trees – from a distance it may not even register as a hedge. To create a shelter belt for a large garden, especially one that backs on to open fields or a busy road, the best choice is a mix of Leylandii conifers

(*Cupressocyparis leylandii*) and European larch (*Larix decidua*).* This provides a fast-growing, very thick hedge, with a hidden advantage. The larches, being deciduous, will filter strong winds during the stormy autumn and winter months, when their branches are bare, while the evergreen conifers will maintain a solid presence. But a thing of beauty it is not.

BUYING AND PLANTING

Hedging plants are usually bought in quantity from specialist hedging nurseries. The cheapest way of buying deciduous hedging plants is as bare-root plants in autumn – this is also the best time for planting. Pot-grown plants available at other times are more expensive. Conifers are sometimes sold as 'root-balled' plants in autumn – these are dug up from the field with a clod of soil clinging to the roots. These should be planted as quickly as possible to avoid 'transplant shock'. Hedging plants are usually available in a range of sizes, and you can expect to pay more for the larger sizes. However, it's not possible to buy full-size hedging plants, so you cannot plant an instant hedge.**

Though clients often want the largest plants, this can prove an unnecessary expense. Small plants often establish more quickly and can grow to the desired size in as little time as more mature ones, which can be slow to establish and fail to put on significant growth in the early years (in this case, it can be just as economical to install a cheap temporary fence, as described previously). However, the recommended spacing for the plants is the same regardless of the size of plant – so a new hedge created with youngsters looks very sparse on planting. Don't forget that you'll need easy access to the hedge to allow for shearing. If the hedge is at the back of a border, incorporate a narrow path next to the hedge behind the planting. For a thick hedge, plant a double row, with the plants arranged in a zigzag.

---

*Leylandii conifers are generally maligned, but they have their uses, this being one of the most appropriate. Their downsides are discussed in greater detail on p. 136.

**Very occasionally, established box hedges are available, but the supply of these cannot be planned for.

Recommended spacings for hedging plants

SPECIES	DISTANCE APART
Berberis	45cm (18in)
Buxus sempervirens (box)	30cm (12in)
Carpinus (hornbeam)	60cm (24in)
Chamaecyparis lawsoniana	60cm (24in)
Crataegus (hawthorn)	45cm (18in)
Cupressocyparis leylandii	75cm (30in)
Elaeagnus	45cm (18in)
Escallonia	45cm (18in)
Fagus sylvatica (beech)	60cm (24in)
Fuchsia	30cm (12in)
Griselinia	45cm (18in)
Ilex aquifolium (holly)	45cm (18in)
Lavandula (lavender)	30cm (12in)
Lonicera nitida	30cm (12in)
Pyracantha (firethorn)	45cm (18in)
Rosa (rose, miniatures)	30cm (12in)
Rosa (rose, shrubs)	60cm (24in)
Rosmarinus (rosemary)	30cm (12in)
Taxus baccata (yew)	60cm (24in)
Thuja plicata	60cm (24in)

Dig over and improve the soil before planting as if preparing to make a lawn (see Chapter 6) – the ground at the perimeter of a site has often been neglected and may be in a poor state. To be sure of planting in a straight line, stretch twine or a piece of washing line, attached to two short stakes, across the length of the hedge. You can actually mark off the planting positions on the twine with a blob of paint or nail varnish. Dig a hole of the appropriate depth for each plant. On root-balled conifers, you'll see a soil mark on the stem just above the roots, indicating how deep the plant was growing in the nursery. It's important to plant to the same depth in the garden.

Peter Anderson

Yew (*Taxus*) is the classic choice for formal hedging and can be clipped with geometric precision.

On planting, most hedging plants should be cut back quite hard, to promote bushiness from low down – otherwise, the hedge develops with a bare base. If you are doing this professionally, clients generally have to be warned (gently) about the gaunt, sparse appearance of a newly planted hedge. It's often forgotten that hedges are plants that need feeding and watering just like other plants. Care of hedges can be an important part of any maintenance contract for professional designers.

EVERGREEN HEDGES

An evergreen hedge provides a solid barrier year-round.

Conifers are generally chosen for tall evergreen hedges. Traditionally, the plant of choice is yew (*Taxus baccata*), which can be clipped hard (and often) to a wall-like appearance or (as Vita Sackville-West preferred at Sissinghurst) left to develop a more feathery surface. It's a myth that yew is slow-growing. It may be a bit reluctant initially, but once established it will easily put on 20cm a year. If this is too grand for the envisaged scheme, try *Thuja occidentalis*, the Western hemlock, which makes a good solid hedge, with no bald patches.

As mentioned before, the much-maligned Leylandii cypress (*Cupressocyparis leylandii*) needs further discussion. Its great advantage is also its biggest (potential) drawback – probably the fastest growing of all conifers, it produces a substantial hedge in only a few years. However, it goes on growing, and before you know it, it is reaching to the sky. Unfortunately, a Leylandii hedge that has been allowed to get out of control is very difficult, if not impossible, to bring back to the desired height. Sawing through the tops leaves a jagged edge that new growth will not conceal. It also tends to die back in patches around the base. If you do choose Leylandii, keep on top of it by cutting it hard *at least* four times a year. The result is a superb hedge with a solid, wall-like appearance.

Peter Anderson

Beech (*Fagus*) is often used for a formal deciduous hedge. Plants retain the faded leaves over most of winter.

For less tall hedges, several evergreens are suitable. Privet (*Ligustrum*) was so widely used around the middle of the twentieth century that it has acquired suburban connotations (along with pampas grass, conifers and heathers). Nevertheless, it has several good points, not the least of which is its tolerance of urban pollution. Though it can be clipped to a firm shape, this is at the expense of the summer flowers (creamy white and rather unpleasantly scented). The varie- gated form is attractive, though not particularly vigorous. The yellow-leaved form (*Ligustrum ovalifolium* 'Aureum') has a tendency to revert to plain green.

Cherry laurel (*Prunus laurocerasus*) and Portugal laurel (*Prunus lusitanica*), the latter with narrower, more elegant leaves, both make good hedges, but do not lend themselves to hard clip- ping to shape. Spotted laurel (*Aucuba japonica* 'Crotonifolia') sounds dreary but does well in shade and, like privet, puts up with pollution. Holly (*Ilex*) makes a superb shiny dark green hedge but can be extremely slow.

Elaeagnus (evergreen varieties) and *Griselinia littoralis* are excellent for coastal gardens, tolerant of salt spray, though neither will grow particularly tall (they can also be used inland, of course). *Elaegnus ebbingei* is particularly attractive, with tough, pewter-grey leaves and sweetly scented (though miniscule) flowers in November. The griselinia has bright green leaves with a unique, soapy texture.

All evergreen hedges can act as supports for climbing plants (providing these are vigorous enough to compete with the hedging but not to the extent that they will swamp it). The flame flower (*Tropaeolum speciosum*), which dies back in winter, makes a spectacular adherent to a yew hedge, the bright scarlet flowers flickering against the dark green background. It is difficult to establish, however, doing best in cool, damp climates and demanding acid soil.

DECIDUOUS HEDGES

If yew is the classic choice for an evergreen hedge, for a deciduous hedge, beech (*Fagus sylvatica*) is often chosen, but I always caution against this. It is slow-growing, and the individual plants within the hedge often grow unevenly. So-called copper beech ('Purpurea') is actually dark purple. A curious feature of beech hedges is that the plants hang on to their faded leaves over winter rather than shedding them (as happens when beech is grown as a free-standing tree). A better bet all round is hornbeam (*Carpinus betulus*), which looks a bit like beech but with slightly narrower leaves, and which is quicker to grow to height.

Both can be given an additional shear in winter, to sensational effect, presenting a mass of twiggy stems with crisply cut edges. In fact, I like the idea of a hornbeam hedge (or indeed any hedge) clipped formally on one face and left shaggy on the other, especially when used to separate a formal area of the garden from an informal one.

TAPESTRY HEDGES

A tapestry hedge comprises a mix of plants, ideally with a similar growth rate – or the more vigorous ones will take over and dominate before the others get into their stride. It differs from a wildlife hedge (see p. 139) in that formal clipping is possible – perhaps even desirable – as it accentuates the different leaf shapes and colours. There's a nice contrast between a clear, formal outline and the more random, 'organic' lines that the individual plants create within the hedge – like a slice cut from a marble cake.*

A combination of yew and box is very subtle, though this is a project for the longer term and can only be achieved with box plants that are of good size on planting (and hence will be expensive). The yews, being naturally taller, will eventually grow above the box, then the stems have to be trained across and tied in to meet.

ORNAMENTAL HEDGES

Apart from their utility function, some hedges have seasonal attraction – usually flowers but also, often, autumn berries. These cannot be clipped formally, as regular pruning would remove some of the flowering wood. Hedges grown for flowers alone should be cut immediately after flowering, then largely left alone (to put on growth for flowering next year). Clip berrying hedges more selectively after flowering, aiming to neaten the plants while retaining as many of the berry-bearing stems as possible.

---

*Although I have seen a more formal solution that involved alternate yellow- and green-leaved forms of Leylandii cypress, all firmly clipped to maintain clear lines between individual plants.

FLOWERING HEDGES	COMMON NAME
Berberis	
Camellia (acid soils only)	
Cotoneaster	
Crataegus	Hawthorn
Pyracantha	Firethorn
Rosa	Rose
Tamarix	Tamarisk
Ulex	Gorse
Viburnum tinus	Laurestine

BERRYING HEDGES	COMMON NAME
Berberis	
Cotoneaster	
Crataegus	Hawthorn
Ilex (females).	Holly
Pyracantha	Pyracantha
Rosa rugosa	Ramanus rose

WILDLIFE HEDGES

Aside from acting as a barrier, a hedge comprising a mix of native plants is a habitat for wildlife – providing not only a food source throughout the year, but a winter shelter. The emphasis on natives is important – these will support a much wider range of fauna, not just birds and small mammals, but all manner of invertebrates that include spiders and mites as well as the obvious pollinating insects. The aim is to develop a self-sustaining eco-system. A wildlife hedge often bounds a wildlife garden, perhaps in conjunction with a garden pond or meadow planting.

Plants with cup-shaped, single flowers will be the most attractive to pollinating insects, as they can easily gain access to the pollen. Berries feed the birds through the winter. Evergreens should be included in the mix to provide cover for birds and hibernating mammals. Hazels (*Corylus*) can be included but have the disadvantage of attracting squirrels – usually considered a pest in such situations as they eat food intended for the birds.

PLANTS FOR A WILDLIFE HEDGE	COMMON NAME
Crataegus monogyna	Hawthorn (flowers and berries)
Ilex	Holly (berries)
Viburnum opulus	Wayfarer tree (flowers and berries)
Acer campestre	Field maple (bark)
Rosa canina	Dog rose (flowers and hips)

Run an ivy through the hedge – the November flowers are a valuable nectar source for bees that are still active at this time of year (on warm, sunny days). If the hedge is a long one, consider adding *Clematis vitalba*, a rampant clematis often known as old man's beard that produces fluffy seed heads that hang on over winter and provide good nesting material for the birds in spring.

A wildlife hedge can never be kept neat in the same way as a formal one. It needs careful pruning at particular times of year to minimize the impact on the wildlife. All the plants need to be allowed to flower. Then you can cut judiciously (but not if the birds are still nesting), retaining as much of the berrying growth as possible, and trimming back other material to ensure that the developing fruits get as much exposure to sun as possible (so they will ripen fully). Cut out older stems and allow new growth to fill in the gaps.

NEGLECTED HEDGES

While you (or a client) may wish to be rid of a straggly, neglected hedge, these can often be brought back into commission by cutting all the growth hard back (best done in late winter to early spring). Individual plants that show signs of die-back within a hedge can also respond well to drastic pruning. However, while old yew hedges can safely be cut back even into bare wood, other conifer hedges will not respond to this treatment. Bare patches near the base of a conifer can be treated cosmetically, if they are not too extensive. Cut out the dead material, then fold over neighbouring live stems to cover the gap (a bit like a comb-over), tying them in position. An overgrown Leylandii hedge is best replaced.

If you do have to replace a hedge, you may also have to replace (or at least improve) the soil, before replanting – if the hedge is growing poorly, it's a sure sign the soil is exhausted.

PLANTS FOR SCREENING

A screen, by implication, is rather more open than a hedge, which is usually clipped regularly. Screening is often used by designers as an instant, or quick, solution – as mature plants can be used – where a barrier or some other windbreak is urgently needed. Dense growth is not looked for, so the plants do not have to be cut back hard initially. Deciduous plants will allow a view through the bare branches in winter.

Airy, twiggy shrubs such as forsythia or cut-leaved elder (*Sambucus racemosa*) do an excellent job and are tolerant of shearing, should this be necessary. Photinias (both evergreen and deciduous) are also excellent (some have bright red spring foliage). Screening is one of the most effective uses of bamboo. But bear in mind that most bamboos are extremely invasive, spreading by vigorous underground runners, and will soon make dense thickets with an accumulation of old canes towards the centre. It may be best to sink them in the ground in large buckets (with holes drilled in the base for drainage). But despite your best efforts, they will still escape through the base – plus, if you are digging large holes for them, you have to dispose of the spoil.

On the large scale, many trees can form an effective screen. A line of closely planted Lombardy poplars looks elegant and makes an effective windbreak when the branches are bare in autumn/winter.

A HEDGE ON STILTS

Pleaching is something of a forgotten art, but worth reviving. In essence, trees, planted in avenues and kept within a certain height, are allowed to develop only a fraction of their side branches, which are ruthlessly trained to the horizontal and tied into the branches of the next tree in the line.

Pleached trees are high maintenance, but look good throughout the year. Once established, the trees present as an airborne hedge (or 'hedge on stilts') when in full leaf in summer, while the tracery of bare stems is almost sculptural in winter, and particularly delightful in early spring as the new leaves emerge. Pleaching allows you to exploit all the principles of proportion (see Chapter 3) within a single planting. Spacing between the individual trees, the proportion of topgrowth to bare trunk and the spaces between each tier should all be precisely calculated. You can further tweak the proportions by planting box to encircle the base of each tree (once established), then trimming this to a precise height – or even allowing the trees to emerge from a box hedge.

Hornbeams (*Carpinus*) can be pleached to form avenues or 'hedges on stilts'.

Only a few subjects lend themselves to this treatment, all deciduous.* Limes (*Tilia*) are the general choice, but hornbeams and beech are also commonly used. Apples, pears and *Sorbus* are worth trying and have the advantage of spring flowers.

A framework is essential. Drive stakes of the desired height of the avenue into the ground to support the trees, spaced about 2–2.5m apart. Attach horizontal battens (or stout wires) to the uprights, about 45cm apart, the lowest one at the desired height of the lowest tier of branches (usually around 1.1m above ground level or slightly higher). Plant a maiden whip (a young tree that comprises a single, flexible upright stem with a scattering of short side branches) against each upright. Tie suitably placed horizontal branches into the framework as they grow. Once the main stem ('leader') reaches above the desired height, bend it over and tie it to the uppermost horizontal batten or wire.

Training is an ongoing process, involving tying in suitably placed growth and ruthless removal of everything else. Once established, badly placed stems have to be cut back once or twice a year to maintain the form – pleaching is not a job for the faint-hearted.

HEDGE LAYING

Laying is a traditional method of keeping hedgerow plants (typically hawthorn) in order and rejuvenating them. It's commonly seen in the English Midlands, and to a somewhat lesser extent in other parts of the country. In late winter, mature upright stems are chopped near ground level

*I once came across a cheat's evergreen version, where the lower trunks of a Leylandii hedge were cleared and the upper portion tightly sheared to give the impression of pleaching.

(though they are not severed right through), then pulled down to an angle close to the horizontal. Whippy side shoots are then woven in to create a low, dense hedge. Upright stakes hold the whole thing together.

This is a job for professionals, who know exactly how hard to make the cuts so that sufficient sap can still flow through the uncut section of stem to keep the plant alive. The beauty of a laid hedge is best appreciated in autumn/winter, when the bare stems present a basket-like appearance.

For obvious reasons, laid hedges are particularly effective in rural gardens, particularly where bounded by open fields, or when used to create a rural touch in urban areas.

DWARF HEDGES

Dwarf hedges don't have a place in every garden – in fact, a dwarf hedge is almost a contradiction in terms, as most are low enough to step over so they hardly create a barrier. But they do give a garden an air of neatness, and often (though not exclusively) tend towards the formal.

The classic choice – especially if you have already opted for yew – is box (*Buxus*). Use this wherever you want a dense, firm hedge with a clear outline. Forget scare stories about box blight that has decimated established hedges in many historic gardens – several modern varieties are immune to the disease. 'Suffruticosa' is best avoided, being both slow-growing and susceptible to disease. Variegated 'Elegantissima' is surprisingly fast-growing. The large-leaved *Buxus sempervirens* will be a tree eventually, if you can project ahead a few centuries. Box hedges can be kept low, to within a height of 30cm and clipped square, but can be also allowed to grow higher, up to 50cm or more, and cut to a point, like a Gothic arch in cross-section.

An alternative to box is an evergreen shrubby honeysuckle, *Lonicera nitida*, though this cannot be clipped to the same firm outline. The yellow form, 'Baggesen's Gold', is best as a foliage plant, unpruned, lighting up a dull area in the depths of winter with its feathery fronds of tiny, old gold leaves.

Lavender or rosemary are traditional choices for a cottage garden, and with these you have a choice. They can be clipped formally like box (though without quite the same firm shape), but this is at the expense of flowers. Allowed to produce their flowers (which will fill the air with bees), plants will splay outwards, concealing the edges of any neighbouring path – which should therefore be wide enough to allow for this. Both these plants tend to go bare at the base after a few years, and cannot be cut hard back to renovate. Old, neglected hedges are best replaced.

An unexpected choice for a flowering hedge is miniature (or patio) roses, which can be pruned with shears early in the season then left uncut and allowed to flower. Even more unusually, grasses can be used to edge a path. These must be the clump-forming types, such as blue fescue (*Festuca glauca*), rather than the spreading, invasive types. The black-leaved *Ophiopogon planiscapus* 'Nigrescens' (not technically a grass but very grass-like) can be dramatic. This, however, must have acid soil.

HARD LANDSCAPING

Here, I confess to being somewhat out of my comfort zone. I have laid paving (not very well) once only, and don't intend doing so again. It's a job best left to contractors if you are short of time. Even so, you need to know how the job should be done – besides, you (possibly in conjunction with a client) will be making all the decisions about materials and the way they are to be used. In your own garden, you may want to have a go yourself if the budget is restricted. Most hard landscaping is intended to be permanent – it will make a major contribution to the scene year round and for many years to come. The area just outside a house is normally given over to hard landscaping and a large proportion of it is likely to be permanently in view. Have an eye not only on how any hard landscaping will look when laid, but how it will age. Durability is a key issue. As with walls, fences and hedges, you often have to balance utility against aesthetic considerations – and sometimes the former will outweigh the latter.

Budgetary considerations

By far the largest part of the budget allocated for this part of a design will be swallowed up by labour costs. A bit of forward planning can help keep these down so that best use is made of workers' time. Materials are heavy (usually) and bulky – and just getting them on site and moving them into position takes up time. Not only will you have to ferry your materials onto the site, but in all probability you'll also be barrowing excavated soil off it, unless this can be used elsewhere. As far as possible, it's best to avoid having to cart material through the house (though this is inevitable if the property is a terraced house with no right of way at the rear). Besides the disruption, only a small volume can be carried through at any one time – and it may not even be possible to use a wheelbarrow to make the job easier. This adds to the time it takes to keep the job in progress.

Many properties do have rear or side access, however. It can sometimes save time if a fence panel can be removed (particularly if the project involves replacing the fence). Considerations such as this may determine how you timetable the making of the garden.

On the subject of budgets, this is one area where it is almost self-defeating to try and cut costs too much by skimping on materials. Granted that the hard landscaping is likely to be in use for many years, you might as well go the distance and invest in something you (or the client, if there is one) really like.* And remember, it will be just as expensive to lay cheap materials as expensive ones, as the length of time needed to complete the job stays the same. Be careful in sourcing your materials. Much 'York' stone is actually imported from the Far East. Though often considerably cheaper than locally quarried stone (for reasons we don't need to go into here), if you are concerned about your carbon footprint, think twice before using this. Some eco-warriors may question the use of natural stone in a garden anyway, as this is not a renewable resource. There are strong arguments for using either reclaimed materials or synthetics, which are either made to resemble naturally occurring stone or announce unashamedly what they are, and not just on the grounds of economy.

Health and safety

The majority of hard landscaping materials are heavy and often awkwardly shaped. Cutting and splitting tools (powered by electricity, petrol or diesel) are potentially hazardous in use. So it goes without saying that you need to equip yourself with the appropriate safety gear – goggles, ear defenders, steel-capped boots, rubberized gloves. Back injuries are the likeliest of all – don't lift any load you can't easily manage.

Planning

The first issue is what the area of hard landscaping is to be used for. (This will also help guide your choice of materials.) Practicality is normally paramount. Paving is often laid just outside a

*If you present your clients with a range of paving options, they will often go for the cheapest – a false economy that you may need tactfully to point out.

house, either as a sitting area or just somewhere to hang out the washing or put the bins. This is inevitably the part of the garden that receives the heaviest use. But even if the space is predominantly functional, careful use of design principles will ensure its visual effectiveness whatever the quality of the materials chosen (see Chapter 3). A patio for sunbathing has to be in full sun in summer, but also screened from prying eyes.

If the planned deck or patio is going to be square or oblong (as it most likely will be) and it's in full view of the house (and vice versa) or adjoins the house, make sure that all angles line up with the house and not with perimeter fences or walls, otherwise it will look very odd. If you have to work with an existing patio that does not align, then try concealing this with planting. If you prefer the edges not to align, this should be a deliberate design choice.

SIZE MATTERS

Be sure to make the area of hard landscaping big enough. Too small, and it will seldom be put to the use for which it was intended. It is, however, always possible to make a small area of hard landscaping larger. An area that has to be large (for instance, to link the house with an outbuilding where the dimensions are already established) presents different problems. An uncompromising sweep of paving or concrete can look like a municipal car park. Here there is scope for breaking up the area, perhaps incorporating a change in level or introducing an island bed. If the area has to remain flat, consider breaking it up visually by combining two or three different materials (e.g. incorporate a line of bricks or cobbles in an area of paving slabs – or use paving slabs of different colours). If you are laying square or oblong slabs, replace a few here and there with cobbles set in concrete, or run lines of brickwork through the space in a decorative pattern.

Spin the plates of function, size and materials simultaneously and aim for them all to land in the same place. The materials chosen must be suitable for the purpose and you will save yourself an awful lot of work if the area is of a size that involves the minimum cutting (particularly of stones, slabs and bricks). If you are using pre-cast slabs, include any gaps you are going to allow between each in your calculations.

Marshalls UK

What could have been a large expanse of paving has been broken up by using different materials in the same colour range.

Materials

Aside from the budgetary constraints, the materials you choose should be appropriate to the site and the adjoining house, quite aside from their intrinsic aesthetic appeal – or make a deliberate contrast. Decking, for instance, has become something of a cliché of suburban gardens, but there are situations where it is without question a suitable choice (see p. 148).

Be wary of using too many different materials within any garden. Confining yourself to one only will certainly ensure unity, but the material itself may be too dominating if used in quantity. Two or at most three provide some variety and can help define (as well as unify) separate areas. On a very practical note, if there is a need to create a new patio that's in full view of a much older, weathered one, either conceal each from the other or unite them visually by running a line of bricks or cobbles around the perimeter of each. Judicious repetition of a particular material can be used to soften unwanted harsh contrasts – unless the contrast itself is to be a strong element of the design. A bold use of stark white concrete can be strikingly effective within the context of reclaimed materials, for instance.

STONE

Natural stone looks beautiful and is exceptionally durable. However, it is often of uneven sizes and thicknesses, making it difficult to cut and to lay (or, more accurately, both jobs will be more time-consuming). Stone is usually very expensive compared to the alternatives. Reconstituted stone is much cheaper and can be virtually indistinguishable from the real thing. On a very purist (even puritanical) note, stone will look best when used strictly within its natural geological belt.* I have come across York paving used right next to Northamptonshire stone, and it is not a happy marriage.

BRICK

If you are going to use bricks for paving in a garden (even if just for edging a path), they must be frost-proof. Most housing bricks are not. Laid flat, these absorb water (being porous), either after rainfall or directly from the ground, and are prone to split when this freezes and expands in winter. Engineering bricks are more durable. However, brick is an exceptionally versatile material and can be laid in a number of decorative patterns – useful for breaking up a large area visually (see also Chapter 8). Reclaimed bricks are readily available.

CONCRETE

Concrete is a much-maligned material, but it earns a place in contemporary design. A perfectly smooth sweep of concrete can be extremely classy, especially in an urban context where no

*The same applies if you are adding rocks to a garden, when creating a rockery or scree. Depending on the location of the garden, local stone may be in short supply and correspondingly expensive.

reference need be made to the outer landscape. Apart from its cheapness, its value rests in its versatility. It can be coloured to the precise shade you want and cast *in situ* – and in whatever shape you want (which eliminates any cutting). Consider using it in a garden where the angles are not true – paving slabs, which inevitably create a straight line, can serve to accentuate any irregularity.

PAVING

Paving slabs are cheap and come in a variety of colours and finishes. They are of uniform size and thickness, so are easy to lay and relatively easy to cut to size. Reclaimed paving slabs are widely available. Most are square or oblong, though you will also find pre-cast ones for laying as circles and other shapes.

COBBLES AND SETTS

Cobbles look terrific set in concrete, but are very uncomfortable underfoot if the area has to be walked on, still less suitable if the area is also intended for tables and chairs which have to be level for stability. In conjunction with other materials, cobbles will effectively break up a larger area. Setts are designed to nest together and can be used as flexible paving (laid direct on sand rather than being cemented in).

GRAVEL AND SLATE

Gravel can be used on top of a membrane on its own or combined with other hard materials. It blends well with plants but is not easy underfoot (or, as with cobbles, for setting chairs and tables on). Though simple to lay, if the membrane does not drain evenly, the gravel will turn green as water collects around it and mosses and lichens take a hold.

DECKING

Decking is due a reappraisal in the same way as concrete and conifers. It is the ideal material to use in a wooded area (and why avoid the obvious?), or in a garden within a housing development that's been made among established trees. It can be equally effective near water – whether it's the sea, a natural stream or canal, or even an artificial garden pond.

Otherwise, decking has the distinct advantages of being cheap, lightweight and easy to lay. And it looks good straight away – smart, in fact, whereas hard paving can look uncompromisingly harsh when freshly laid. Use it where a lawn would be impractical (for instance in a heavily shaded garden) or to terrace a gentle slope. As with a timber fence, owing to the nature of the material, decking is much less durable than other forms of hard landscaping.

RAILWAY SLEEPERS

Railway sleepers are reclaimed and are ideal for making raised beds and steps, possibly in conjunction with gravel or decking. They have nearly always been treated with a wood preservative and this should not be allowed to come into contact with soil. The preservative will leach into the soil, causing potential damage to plant roots and invertebrate soil organisms. To avoid this, the sleepers should be laid on lengths of impermeable material (such as a pond liner). If you are using them to make raised beds, line the interior of the bed with pond liner (held in place with rust-proof nails or staples) before filling with soil. If you need to cut them to size, treat the exposed ends with a timber preservative.

Building a patio

If the patio or terrace is to meet the house, building regulations require that the surface should be at least 15cm below the damp-proof course (which you'll easily identify if the house is brick-built) where it meets the house wall.

PREPARING THE SITE

Mark out the site with strings and pegs, checking that the corners make right angles using a builder's square (there are more details on measuring in Chapter 10). The strings should be at the height of the finished patio – they will act as a guide when you come to lay the paviors. To do the job properly, the patio should slope gently away from the house, so that rainwater will not run back towards the brickwork.* (Ideally, any patio created in a garden should slope slightly so that excess water will run off freely, preferably into a flower bed or border.)

Dig out the site. (You can save any reusable topsoil but skip the subsoil, unless this is included in your plans – for instance, to create a mound or rock garden.) You need to allow for a 10cm layer of hardcore or scalpings topped by a 5cm layer of building sand – topped by the thickness of the slabs.** Remove all traces of weeds (most of which are quite capable of growing through cement). For belt and braces, apply a weedkiller over the site. Consolidate the ground at the base by stamping all over it or using a whacker plate (which is where the ear defenders come in). You might put down a membrane at this point, to guard against weed growth, but it must be permeable to allow excess water to drain through.

Barrow in a 10cm layer of hardcore or scalpings, then tamp this down. Check the level then top with a 5cm depth of building sand – also tamped down.

*A suitable, unobtrusive drop is 2.5cm over 2m. To achieve this, hammer a peg into the ground so that the top is at the desired level. Some 2m away, hammer in a second peg. Lay a straight plank across two pegs, then drive in the second (hammering through the plank) until the plank is level (use a spirit level to check). Remove the plank. Place a 2.5cm chock of wood on top of peg 2, then replace the plank. Hammer peg 2 again until the plank is level. Remove the plank and the chock, then run the string from the top of peg 1 to the top of peg 2 (which now sits lower in the ground).

*This represents the minimum depth of excavation. This footing is suitable for most domestic use, but not for hard standing for a car – which is a job for a builder. On soft or peaty soil, dig a foundation 5cm deeper.

LAYING THE SLABS

Assuming the patio butts up against the house, start at the house end and set out the row of slabs. If the patio is within the garden and free-standing, start at the slightly raised end (this may be next to a wall or fence). Stand on a plank laid on the sand, if this is necessary, to spread your weight. If you've done your sums correctly, you should find that the slabs all fit neatly without any need for cutting. If there have to be narrow gaps between them, use spacers – narrow strips of wood – to make sure they are all the same (as with tiling a bathroom wall).

After laying the paving, brush dry mortar into the spaces between the slabs.

Once you're happy with the first row and satisfied they are all level, they can be mortared into position. Lift the first slab and, with a bricklayer's trowel, lay four strips of mortar in a box shape, slightly smaller than the slab. For extra stability (especially if the slabs are large), make a central cross of mortar or dab a blob of mortar in the middle of the box. (This is what you're supposed to do – but most people just dab on the mortar in five blobs, as on a die.) Set the slab on top of the mortar and firm it down to the appropriate level (following the line marked by the string). Lay the rest of the row before starting on the second.

Unless rain is forecast, hose down the newly paved area.

After laying the slabs, leave them for a couple of days for the mortar to harden. If you have allowed spaces between slabs, brush dry mortar over them to fill them. Brush off any excess, then either give the whole area a light sprinkle with a hose or just allow rainfall and any moisture in the atmosphere to do the job for you.

The same method can be used for laying stone. But here you will have to adjust the depth of the sand as you work to accommodate any variation in thickness. Although paving slabs can be cut to fit into awkward corners (and even into curves), I have a problem with the further cutting of quarried stone. Respecting the integrity of the material, it can be more sympathetic to lay the stones as they are and fill in any gaps with gravel or cobbles. It may be necessary to lay out all the stone first before mortaring in to achieve a satisfying balance if you have to add a second material.

OASE (UK) Ltd

A sympathetic use of decking – next to water

Decking

In many respects, decking represents the easy option and is much quicker to lay than slabs, as the material is lighter and much easier to cut. Unlike paving, however, it requires regular maintenance, and may have to be replaced after a couple of years – though that at least allows for some flexibility in the design. Wooden decking tends to be slippery, even slimy, when wet – ultimately, decking belongs in a dry climate, though you may find yourself compelled to use it if there are no obvious alternatives.

By its very nature, decking can make a strong impact on the design – if you think about what it actually is. This is an aspect that is often overlooked. In essence, a deck comprises a series of planks of wood laid parallel on top of a frame. Usually, the surface is riven or grooved, to provide a secure footing in use. Its very fabric, therefore, imposes straight lines on the design, and this can be used to your advantage. Depending on which direction the timbers are laid, the lines can either accentuate length or width. They can make a long, narrow space look wider and shorter, and vice versa. To break up a large area of deck, consider laying the timbers in different directions, some straight, some at right angles, some diagonal – especially if you are creating a series of linked decks. Don't get too carried away, though – the result should still be harmonious and easy on the eye. Decking 'tiles' can be used to make paths or steps.*

It's essential that all the timbers are dry before you start work and that the deck is made during dry weather (during a warm spell in summer is the ideal time). As a natural material, it swells when wet and shrinks when dry. Lay the timbers loosely initially and give them a few days to dry out further before screwing them into position (using corrosion-resistant screws). This allows for expansion during wet weather.

If space allows, it's usually easiest to make the framework for the deck on a separate area of hard standing, such as a patio or driveway, then manoeuvre it into position rather than making it *in situ*.

MAKING THE DECK

Dig a foundation, allowing for a 10cm layer of hardcore or scalpings. Remove all traces of weeds and apply a weedkiller to the ground. Compact the soil, then barrow or shovel in the hardcore. Tamp this down. Lay a weed-suppressing (but water-permeable) membrane over the area and hold this down with a thin layer of grit or shingle.

Make a framework for the decking timbers, slightly smaller than the proposed deck. The framework consists of a series of joists that run parallel to each other screwed to planks at each end that tie the structure together. Space the joists about 40cm apart. Screw in angle brackets or joist hangers in the corners (where the ends of joists meet the plank) for extra stability and to keep the shape true. Screw all the joists to one end plank first, then attach the other plank on the opposite side. Check the level at all stages. For the ultimate in solidity, attach noggins (cross pieces or bracing pieces) 40cm apart between each joist, staggering them between consecutive bays.

Lay the framework on the foundation. Ideally, the joists should be supported on bricks or slabs – alternatively, hammer in a series of posts to either side of each joist to hold them in position. Set the decking planks at right angles to the supporting joists. They should overhang slightly at the edges. If you have to cut the planks within the deck, the cut ends should meet over a joist.

*Depending on the situation and the intended use, to prevent slips when wet these tiles can be finished with an aggregate, or a fine mesh chicken wire can be stretched over them. But these coatings are not very sympathetic under bare feet.

Leave a gap of about 6mm between successive planks to allow for expansion. Most wood sold for decking will have been pressure-treated to preserve it against wet, but you will need to paint all cut ends with a wood preservative or sealant.

For the most economical use of the material (if you are on a tight budget), decking should be laid diagonally across the frame – this enables you to make best use of the offcuts.

If the deck is to adjoin the house, fix the framework to a ledger board – a horizontal timber attached to the house supported on spacers drilled into the brickwork (to allow for ventilation).

Steps

Steps are almost essential on steeply sloping ground, but can also be used on more gentle gradients. To measure a slope, you need to calculate the drop over a given distance (see Chapter 10). Beautiful steps are the mark of a good designer. How often have you had to use steps outdoors where you either have to lengthen or shorten your stride or feel that you are going to plummet down them?

Steps comprise risers (the vertical bit) and treads (the flat bit). To be easy to negotiate, the depth of the tread added to twice the riser should equal about 65cm (it's impossible to be more prescriptive owing to the difference in most people's length of stride – but this should be suitable for most). In practice, this means that the longer the tread is the shallower the riser should be. (This proportion gives a much more generous tread than builders use for staircases in houses, which are generally of necessity much steeper so they occupy the minimum ground space – it's assumed that your progress through a garden will be more leisurely.)

It is critical that all the steps in any flight are the same size – or users will miss their footing or even slip a disc. However, a very long staircase could incorporate a landing (even, dare I say it, a *deck*) mid-way, possibly acting as a resting place or viewing platform if it can be made large enough. Most steps are no use for lawnmowers. If steps are to descend to a lawn, you may need to make a second, sloping service path (concrete is the best material), screened or planted out of view.

MAKING STEPS ON SLOPING GROUND

To mark out steps on a sloping site, drive a series of pegs into the ground to each side of the proposed flight (a pair to either side for each step), and run a string between them, pulled taut. Run horizontal strings between successive pairs to mark the front of each tread. Check that the horizontals are level using a spirit level. Using the strings as a guide, dig out the steps and compact the soil with your feet.

Starting from the bottom, dig out a footing about 15cm deep for the lowest riser. (To make the risers, use engineering bricks, cut down railway sleepers or treated timbers.) Put in a 7cm layer of hardcore then top this with concrete. Once this has hardened, position the riser (a length of timber can be held in position with short posts at each end). Check the level of each riser as you proceed. Backfill the space behind with scalpings, then lay a slab for the tread over it. To allow for water run-off, the tread should overhang the riser and should slope slightly towards the edge (but not so steeply that it tips you off). Lay the next riser at the back of the tread, then continue to work up the flight.

If the steps are going to have deep treads, you could even make them out of decking. For a very relaxed look – especially effective in a woodland area – consider using railway sleepers for the risers and simply dig out shallow treads, line them with membrane, then top with chipped bark or gravel. This also eliminates the need to cut paving to fit.

Paths

Paths lead from one part of the garden to another – if that sounds blindingly obvious, it's worth pointing out that you cannot guarantee that people will necessarily stick to a path if another route suggests itself. A winding path through a lawn won't stop people from running across it – and you may well see a self-made mud path emerge on a grassed area even when there's a perfectly good paved one near to it, if the paved one offers a longer way round. The best paths are usually straight and only curve where they absolutely have to.

Again, practical matters should guide planning. A path should be at least 1m wide if a wheel-barrow or lawnmower is going to have to be pulled along it. Twice this width will allow two people to walk side by side along it (narrow paths can be lonely, but are sometimes unavoidable in a small garden, especially if you are keeping a close eye on proportions). If a path runs along or between borders, remember that plants will flop over in summer, narrowing paths even further and wetting ankles after a shower.

LAYING FLEXIBLE PAVING

Dig out the area to a depth of 20cm, firm the base, then fill with a 10cm layer of scalpings. Tamp this down then spread over a 5cm layer of building sand. Also tamp this down firmly. Define the edge with bricks or blocks or timbers nailed to short posts driven into the ground. Check the level. Starting at one end, fill in the area, laying the paving blocks or setts directly onto the sand.

Dare I say that your measurements have to be exact when working with these materials – the individual cobbles should butt tightly up against each other with no gaps in between. If you make a mistake, even out the gaps across the area, then fill with mortar. But then the paving is 'flexible' no longer.

10

SIMPLE DRAUGHTING

This chapter deals with draughting only at its most basic, but should be adequate for most domestic gardens. For a very large site with many changes of level, it's worth employing a surveyor to do some of the work for you.

Draughting is the process by which you express all your design ideas, usually on a single, two-dimensional plan.* In principle, this plan is a stand-alone document that can easily be understood by all. In practice, that entails the use of certain conventions, which are the subject of this chapter. What follows may seem offputtingly technical, even tedious. But if you are working for a client, it's essential that you have a detailed plan from which to work. Even if you are only designing your own garden, it's a useful exercise, and it is worth approaching this in exactly the same way as if you were doing it professionally. The draughting process is instructive in itself, as the systematic approach it demands generally helps clarify your ideas – sometimes, it's in the very act of measuring and drawing that you realize what will and won't be

*Scale models – needed for very elaborate schemes that may involve building work – are not dealt with here.

possible in any given garden. The use of the term 'process' is deliberate. There is a series of stages between measuring the site and producing the plan. If these seem like prescriptive rules, bear in mind that they represent only one way of achieving the desired outcome, and with experience you may evolve your own preferred methods of working.

Your finished plan needs to be as comprehensive as possible but simple – add detail only if strictly necessary. Bear in mind that your design may need to be modified at a later stage and also that it may not be realized all in one go – the work may be spread over several 'campaigns'. From your perspective, it's an aide-mémoire, and you'll have a whole bundle of preliminary sketches and lists to support it that you can refer to should this be necessary when work is in progress. If you are doing this professionally, it will be the only thing that the client and the contractor ever get to see, so it needs to represent a complete view of your vision of the garden. Your intentions should be clear.

There's another important reason for keeping things simple if you are producing a design for a client. Essentially, your job is to make a garden and it's in that that most of the budget should rest. Your plan should look like something that has not taken an excessive amount of time to produce, rather than being a piece of very elaborate artwork. It's a fine balance. You can suggest planting and paving without drawing in every single flower and paving stone. On the other hand, many clients experience difficulties in conjuring up in their minds a three-dimensional reality from a fairly styl-ized two-dimensional plan – hence the value of including a cross section, elevation or perspective drawing (see below) that is more inspirational and conveys your creativity as designer.

In essence, draughting is a straightforward process, but it can be very time-consuming – indeed, it should be. Time taken in the initial stages – measuring the site, making preliminary sketches and drawing up lists – invariably pays off longer term. At first sight, the work involved in drawing up even a very simple site seems daunting, but think of this – you need to find a way to unlock your creativity and at some point you will be confronted by a blank sheet of paper. The process of making a plan is systematic, not creative, and the tiny amount of creativity needed to create a successful garden emerges only towards the end. Don't be discouraged by this if you think you can't draw – there are ways round it, as will emerge later on.

Your first task is to create a record of the site *as you found it*. Once you start work, any existing garden will rapidly vanish and you then have no reference to what was there before you began. By all means take photographs as well, though these can be of limited use, depending on how much you can fit into the viewfinder.

You'll make a series of drawings – none of which you show the (hypothetical) client – as you progress towards the finished design.

Equipment

You do not need a vast amount of equipment to design a garden.

On site, a retracting measuring tape in a circular case is essential. Most are made of fibreglass. One of 30m is suitable – those with 100m reach are useful for measuring a large site, but are expensive and can be difficult to manipulate if you are working solo. You'll also need stout stakes or pegs, a mallet (for hammering these into the ground), some straight canes and strong string or twine. A tent peg or skewer is useful for securing the end of the tape into the ground. A spirit level is needed for measuring sloping ground and generally for checking levels.

For producing the plan once indoors, a dedicated architect's drawing board that can be raised, lowered and angled would be nice, but is by no means essential – a kitchen table will serve almost as well. A T-square is needed to draw right angles as are a pair of compasses for transferring measurements using triangulation (see p. 159). The type with an extending arm is best. A scale rule is used for drawing to scale. In cross-section, this useful bit of kit looks like a propeller or the business end of a wind turbine. It thus has six edges, each marked with a different scale. A typical model measures 33cm in length with scales of:

1:500
1:1000
1:1250
1:1500
1:2000
1:2500

If you decide to draw your plan at a scale of 1:50, use the 1:500 edge, and the 1:1000 for 1:100. Use a set of French curves or a flexi-curve ruler for drawing curves. Finally, you'll need sharp pencils in a gradation of hardnesses (you'll end up mostly using the one that responds best under the pressure of your hand), an eraser, fine-tipped felt pens and some means of adding colour – watercolours, inks or (simpler) felt-tip pens. Correction fluid and a glue stick can be a god-send, even in this digital age.

The site survey

You have already carried out an assessment of the site (see Chapter 2) – and, if you are working professionally, will have made notes about certain aspects of it that you have discussed with the client. Some of these will find their way on to the site inventory (see p. 163).

Start by making a rough sketch of the site overall that includes the back of the house. Mark in all the boundaries, paths, patios, beds and borders, sheds and established trees – exactly what you see in front of you. This drawing does not have to be to scale, but it does need to be comprehensive. It represents an important stage in the design process, as you'll use this to record all the measurements necessary for drawing up the base plan (see p. 164). Use a sheet of A4 (or A3 for a larger garden) attached to a clipboard, possibly with a second sheet for recording all the measurements.

MEASURING

The process of measuring a site in itself offers one of the best ways of getting to grips with the project, perhaps even more so than the site assessment. Measure all the elements drawn on your sketch. Be systematic in recording all the measurements and write them down in the order you make them, labelling the sketch as you go. All measuring is most easily accomplished with a second pair of hands – preferably not the client's (though you may have no choice). If any distance exceeds the length of your tape measure, stretch this to its fullest extent, then attach twine to the end. Extend this to the point you wish to measure to, then measure this extra length and add it to the length of the tape. Alternatively, drive a stake into the ground at the tape's furthest extent, rewind, then make an additional measurement with the tape (making sure that you maintain a straight line). Always use metric, which you'll find far easier when you come to scale down measurements on the base plan.

First, measure the side of the house facing the garden – it isn't going anywhere, and will be the same at the end of the project as when you started. (Where possible, use this as your starting point for all future measurements within the garden.) Identify a series of points (e.g. corner A to doorframe B; doorframe to doorframe, B–C; doorframe to window, C–D, etc.) that will be straightforward to measure. Identify these points on the sketch. As you measure each, mark each measurement on the sketch. If you need to add detail, make a separate sketch of that part of the house. Alternatively, create a separate list of the measurements – e.g. AB = 1.1m (or whatever the distance is) – to the side, or on a second sheet of paper.

Measure and mark on your drawing the position of all doorways and windows – and how they open. It's good practice also to measure the drop below ground-floor window frames (why this is so will become clear later). The back of the house thus becomes a clearly identifiable point of reference from which many of the remaining measurements can be taken.

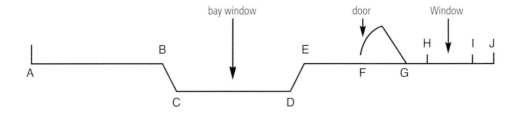

Make as many measurements as you can, even if this seems excessive – it will ensure the accuracy of your base plan.* Work your way methodically around the site, either clockwise or anticlockwise as suits you.

*By the time you have finished, you may well have run through the alphabet several times – use A1–B1 to start the second round, and so on.

If the back of the house is irregular – that is, if there is a bay window to a sitting room or a porch – this can be measured in one of two ways. Either establish a baseline on site with stakes and string or use offsetting (see p. 160). To create a baseline, pull a string taut between two stakes driven into the ground – in this case, parallel to the house. Using triangulation (see below), plot the position of each stake so that you will be able to add the line to your sketch. Measure off the edge of the bay as shown below. (If the bay is curved, use a series of canes laid against the base-line as described for measuring a curved path.)

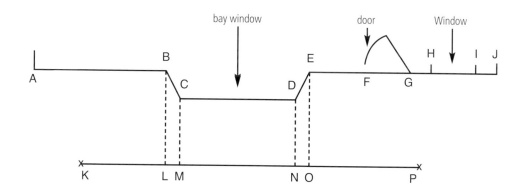

The value of all this measuring – apart from enabling you to recreate it on the base plan – is that you may well find suitable pleasing proportions within the building itself that can be used when you come to create your design.

Having measured the house, you now need to measure from it all the elements that will be retained – effectively, the boundaries and anything that can't be changed, such as garage, shed, manhole cover or oil tank, as well as any mature trees and shrubs that will be part of the new garden.

TRIANGULATION

Triangulation is a means of establishing the exact position of an object in the garden using two other fixed points as reference.

As an example: to plot the position of a tree, choose a fixed point on the house (e.g. the corner or the doorframe edge) whose position you have already recorded. Measure from here to the tree. Select a second fixed point (such as a window frame), then measure from here to the tree. You have effectively measured a triangle, the base being between the two fixed points, the apex being the tree. You will be able to reproduce this on the base plan using compasses (see p. 165).

Use triangulation to plot the boundaries of the site, even if the garden presents as a uniform square or oblong. What appear to be right angles are seldom exact, as you may discover to your cost if you need to pave an area of the garden only to discover that a square or oblong slab will not fit into the corner.

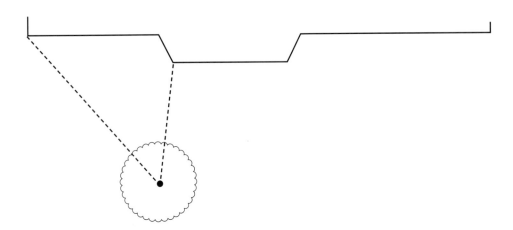

OFFSETTING

Offsetting involves taking measurements at right angles to a straight line. That straight line may be an existing element (such as the back of the house or a fence) or may be a baseline that you create yourself by running a string between two stakes. Offsetting is often an alternative to triangulation and can be simpler, though in practice it is slightly less accurate. Use offsetting to mark the position of features that are near the house, such as a manhole cover in a patio.

To revisit the example of the tree – if this is relatively near the house, simply measure directly from the house wall. Make sure the tape meets the house at a right angle. Measure also from that point on the house to the nearest recorded point – such as the corner of the house or the doorframe. These measurements should be sufficient to allow you to draw the tree on the plan in the correct place.

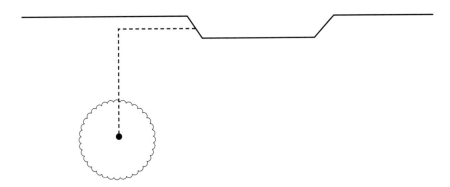

You can also use offsetting to record the curve of a path. Create a baseline (as described above) from one end of the curve to the other (record the end points using triangulation). Lay a series of canes along the line at right angles to it and at 1m intervals. Measure the distances from the line to the edge of the path.

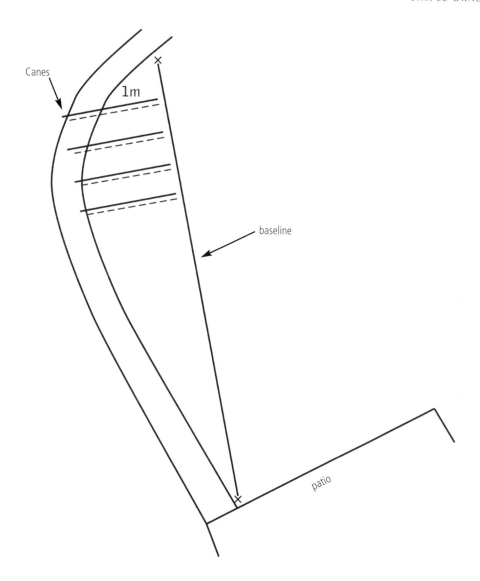

Canes

1m

baseline

patio

Use the same method to plot an irregular boundary or to establish the position of a round, oval or kidney-shaped bed. Either set up a (temporary) baseline nearby or measure from a nearby fence or wall (if there is one), whose position is easy to plot.

OTHER MEASUREMENTS

It's not absolutely essential, but it may also be worth measuring the height of the house (up to the eaves, excluding the roof) – especially if you want to create a patio next to it in a particular proportion (see Chapter 3). Some idea of the height of the house is also useful for judging the length of the shadow it casts in mid-summer. If the house is brick-built, count the number of courses (say forty), then divide by a convenient number (say four) to give a number of courses that you can easily measure (e.g. ten). Measure the height of the ten courses, then multiply by four to give the height of the house. Alternatively, count the number of courses within a given height – say, 1m. Then add up the number of courses to the eaves, then divide by the number of courses in a single metre to produce the height in metres.

If the house is not made of brick (or if the bricks have been rendered), place a cane of known length (say 2m) against the wall, then take a photograph of the whole house from a good distance. You should then be able to estimate the height of the house reasonably accurately using the cane as a scale. If you don't want to use photography (or can't get the whole elevation in the viewfinder), simply make a rough estimate by eye, using the cane as a guide – that is, you calculate the number of canes that would fit between the ground and the eaves. This is not exact by any means, but good enough for most purposes.

Use the same system to measure the height of a tree that is to be retained. Also measure the extent of the tree's canopy. Of necessity, this is usually approximate, but will help when you consider the placements of ponds, decks and flower beds at the design stage.

You might also record – roughly – the position of trees and buildings outside the garden that have an impact on the space (and about which you can do nothing). These will not feature in the finished drawing, but they may need to be listed on the site inventory (see below).

RECORDING A SLOPE

Sloping ground presents the designer with certain problems. If the garden has a slight, almost imperceptible slope, you can just make a note of this in the site inventory (see p. 163). A uniform, very gentle slope may not make much difference to a meadow or flower bed, but will be obvious if you are planning to add a large pond or deck, which will be level. You can sometimes judge a gentle slope by eye, if there is an element nearby that you know to be straight, such as brickwork in a wall or a fence panel, and the slope runs horizontally against it.

Otherwise, to measure the drop in sloping ground, drive a tall stake into the ground at the foot of the slope. Stretch a string from the top of the slope (fixed to the ground with a tent peg) to the stake. Pull the string taut and tie it to the stake so that the string is level (check with a spirit level). Measure the distance from the base of the cane to the point at which you have tied the string (A), then measure the length of the string from the cane to the tent peg (B). These figures give you the drop (A) over the distance (B). For a more extended or irregular slope, you can insert canes at regular intervals (say every 2m) down the slope then measure between them.

To a greater or lesser degree, these measurements offer an approximation only, but will still enable you to calculate the volume of soil that needs to be moved (or imported) should this be necessary to level the site (particularly if any spoil will have to be skipped).

An alternative method, for a more accurate reading, is to use a length of clear plastic hosepipe. Fix this to stakes at the top and bottom of the slope and fill with water (which always finds its own level). The difference between the heights of the water columns tells you the drop.

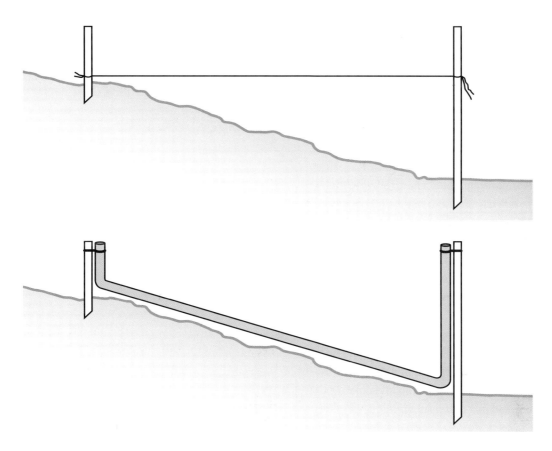

Site inventory

This is no more than a list of all the things you have identified (with the client, if there is one) that you are looking to improve. Though it can be note-like, it should be comprehensive. Approach it as a list of negatives – all the elements of the site that you want to change. You may wish to photograph all of these, as a reminder. This list does not appear on the finished plan – in fact, you may not even need to show it to a client, if these are things already agreed.

A typical list might include the following (and this list is by no means exhaustive):

✓ Fence in poor condition
✓ Overgrown tree
✓ Flower beds too small
✓ Soil in poor condition
✓ Lawn drains badly
✓ Pond poorly sited
✓ Patio too small/broken slabs
✓ Garage an eyesore

Site analysis

To some extent this mirrors and amplifies the site inventory and encapsulates all the tasks you're going to undertake to improve the site. Unlike the inventory, it is positive – a 'to do' list. A comprehensive list will greatly help with planning your time and budgeting:

✓ Replace fence
✓ Cut down or reduce size of tree
✓ Extend existing flower beds
✓ Improve soil
✓ Improve lawn
✓ Fill in pond
✓ Extend/repair/replace patio
✓ Add planting to screen garage

Add everything else you're going to do (and have discussed with the client):

✓ Create moving water feature
✓ Incorporate meadow planting into lawn
✓ Replant shrub border for winter interest
✓ Exploit microclimate offered by house wall with suitable plants

Creating the base plan

The base plan is your drawn record of the site as it is at present. It reproduces to scale all the measurements taken on site and forms the basis for all future drawings.

Stick a sheet of gridded paper to the drawing board with masking tape. This will merely be a guide for drawing straight lines and marking right angles – the scale of the grid is immaterial. Lay a sheet of tracing paper over this, on which you will draw the base plan.

Decide on a suitable scale for your design. Ultimately, you will ideally want to fit the whole garden (and garden side of the house) on one sheet (usually A1 or A2), allowing room at the side to record other relevant information (see 'Title block', p. 178) and for a cross-section, elevation or perspective drawing (see p. 171). Select the scale that will allow you to create as large a drawing of the site as possible. It's not unlikely that you'll find it best to draw the site at an angle rather than square on the sheet – you can draw a long, narrow garden bigger if you set it on the diagonal. Rotate the sheet of tracing paper over the grid to the desired angle so that you can continue to use the grid as a guide for straight lines.

Following your preliminary sketch, draw the site on the sheet, using the scale rule. Transfer each measurement in the order that you recorded it on site. If you chose to order them as a list, this is where its value becomes obvious, as you can cross off each measurement as you go. You may find that some measurements are incorrect, if lines will not meet. Return to the site if necessary to check any that are obviously wrong. If you are planning your own garden, you can just step outside – otherwise, make a separate list of measurements that need confirming so you only need to revisit the client once.

Use compasses to replicate measurements taken using triangulation. The base of the triangle will already have been drawn (if, for instance, you measured from the house). To establish the position of the apex, using the scale rule, open your compasses to the scaled-down distance from one of the base's corners to the apex. Place the point of the compasses in the base of that corner on the drawing, then mark a pencil arc roughly where the apex should be. Do the same for the other corner. Where the arcs cross is the apex of the triangle you measured on site – the position of the hypothetical tree referred to previously.

Using the above method, draw in any baselines you set up on site, then use these to reproduce all measurements that you took using offsetting. The series of canes that you used to record a curve thus becomes a series of lines, the tips of which you can join together using a French curve (or flexi curve), thus reproducing the curve. Once this is drawn in, you can rub out the baseline and the secondary lines.

At the end of the exercise, you have a drawing that is covered with pin pricks and rubbings out. Depending on the extent of the corrections, it may even be quite messy – but its accuracy is far more important than visual appeal. Trace the drawing through onto a fresh sheet of tracing paper. Alternatively, clean up any ugly marks with correction fluid then photocopy it. This copied version is the base plan. Never make any alterations directly onto this plan – because, along with any photographs you have taken and your own notes, it serves as your record of the site. Once you have the base plan, you can dispense with the sheet of gridded paper that has underlaid it. You may well use a grid to help create your design, but this is dealt with below.

Designing

Lay a fresh sheet of tracing paper over the base plan. First, bring through on to the design all the elements that are to be retained – the house, obviously, and any hard landscaping, paths and trees that have to stay. At this point, you might like to make several copies or photocopies of this plan – or at least one – so you don't need to keep repeating this aspect of the job should you have a radical change of heart once you are halfway through (or indeed if a client rejects any part of your finished design) and you find yourself, literally, back at the drawing board. File away the base plan, which is now needed for reference only.

This is the point at which you start actually designing the garden – which can be an exciting, if sometimes alarming, moment. This is the point at which you begin to unlock your creativity. A good way to begin is with a list of all your (or the client's) requirements – a wish list of the things you want to incorporate in the garden. Simply as a preliminary exercise, draw them on the plan as a series of rough 'bubbles' of the approximate size without worrying too much about exact placement. Tick them off on the list as you go. This should give you an immediate sense of whether everything will fit into the available space. For instance, if you see that there is insufficient room to include both a pond and a wildflower planting, now would be the time to reconsider or point this out to the client. Once you have a feel for how the whole scheme will work, you can start drawing with greater precision. If you are nervous about drawing, remember that this is a process – you do not have to achieve a finished design all at once. Rub out unsuccessful parts as you go, or stick pieces of paper over them – you can always make a new clean tracing (or photocopy) of the plan once you are happy.

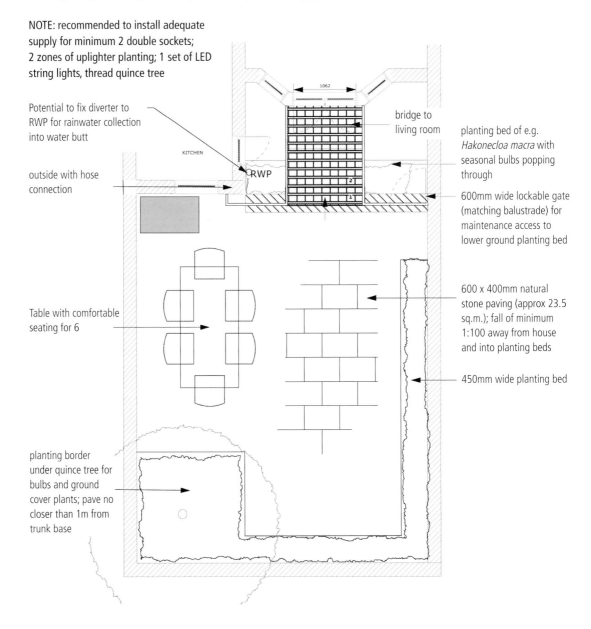

NOTE: recommended to install adequate supply for minimum 2 double sockets; 2 zones of uplighter planting; 1 set of LED string lights, thread quince tree

Potential to fix diverter to RWP for rainwater collection into water butt

outside with hose connection

Table with comfortable seating for 6

planting border under quince tree for bulbs and ground cover plants; pave no closer than 1m from trunk base

KITCHEN

RWP

bridge to living room

planting bed of e.g. *Hakonecloa macra* with seasonal bulbs popping through

600mm wide lockable gate (matching balustrade) for maintenance access to lower ground planting bed

600 x 400mm natural stone paving (approx 23.5 sq.m.); fall of minimum 1:100 away from house and into planting beds

450mm wide planting bed

Always include an arrow to indicate north. There are certain conventions about how to draw plants and other features – they offer quite a good means of conveying information (e.g. the number of plants to be used in a hedge) with the minimum amount of drawing. When adding in trees, indicate the extent of the canopy.

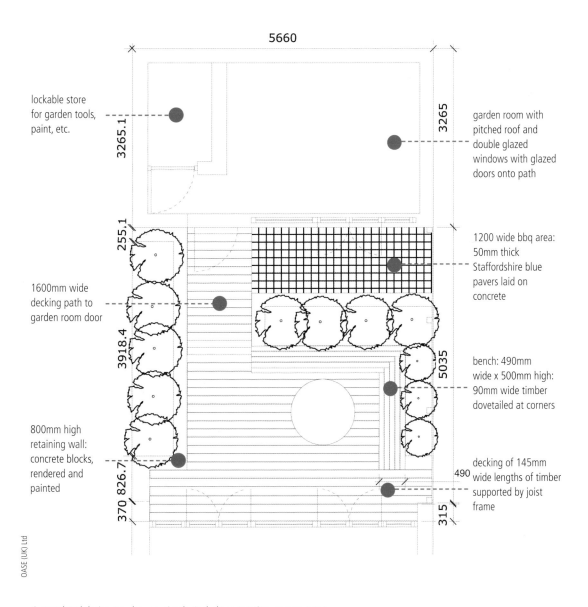

A completed design may be very simple. Include annotation, as necessary.

167

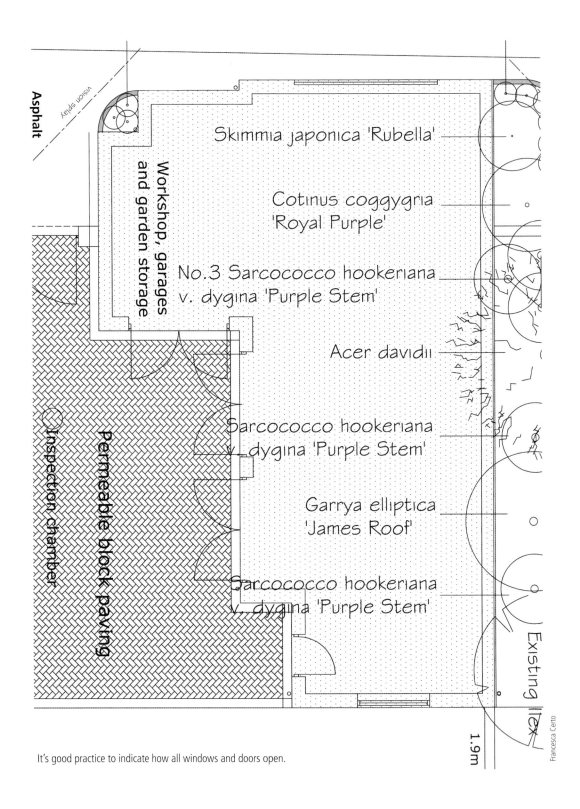

Asphalt

vision splay

Workshop, garages
and garden storage

Inspection chamber

Permeable block paving

Skimmia japonica 'Rubella'

Cotinus coggygria
'Royal Purple'

No.3 Sarcococco hookeriana
v. dygina 'Purple Stem'

Acer davidii

Sarcococco hookeriana
v. dygina 'Purple Stem'

Garrya elliptica
'James Roof'

Sarcococco hookeriana
v. dygina 'Purple Stem'

Existing Ilex

1.9m

Francesca Certo

It's good practice to indicate how all windows and doors open.

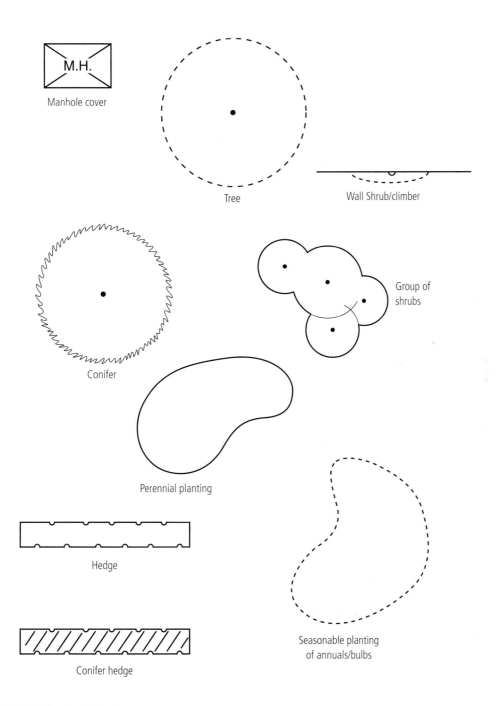

M.H.

Manhole cover

Tree

Wall Shrub/climber

Conifer

Group of shrubs

Perennial planting

Hedge

Seasonable planting of annuals/bulbs

Conifer hedge

Symbols for indicating plants, etc.

USING A GRID

Many designers find it easiest to draw to a grid. A grid allows you to assess measurements easily (using the scale rule) and also helps plan proportions (particularly if you are adding in hard landscaping or decking) and achieve a good balance of the required elements in the design. Draw your own grid (to the chosen scale) on tracing paper and tape this between the base plan and the sheet you are designing on. If you line the grid up with the house wall, it will be immediately apparent to what extent the boundaries are true. The elements you add to the design do not necessarily have to fit into the grid exactly – it is merely a guide.

You can base the grid on 1m or 2m squares, reduced to the scale you are using. Less usually (but sometimes more effectively), you can opt instead for a 'bastard' measurement, perhaps based on one of the measurements taken from the house – for instance, the drop below the sitting room window or the width of the back door (most standard doors measure between 80cm and 90cm, so your grid could be based on that). The grid thus becomes less of a measuring device and more of a design tool that can help produce unity between house and garden based on proportion. Any elements that fit into this grid exactly (e.g. a path, patio or flower bed) will have a subtle relationship with the house.

Note that use of a grid in no way assumes that any element you put in the design will be square or rectangular – circles, ovals and kidney-shapes can all fit into a grid, as well as even more random shapes.

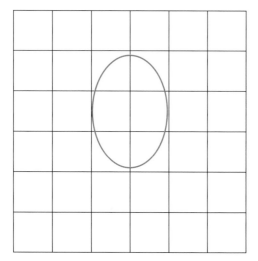

An oval can be fitted into a grid.

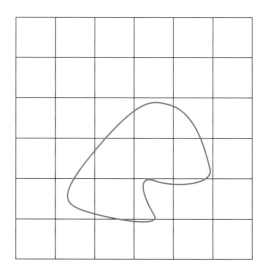

Use a grid to give pleasing proportions to what are at face value random shapes.

If you do choose to line up the grid with the house, it's then easy to draw in patios and paths that are parallel or at right angles to the house. But you may find this strategy unnecessarily restrictive, as it almost inevitably leads to a geometric approach. In this case, try swivelling the grid round 45 degrees so it presents diagonally.

Cross-sections, elevations and perspective drawings

A sketch of a small area of the garden – possibly with colour – brings a flat, two-dimensional design to life. This part of the plan is often what sells a design to a client – if they are in two minds about proceeding with the project, it may help persuade them. It is not strictly necessary if you are merely designing your own garden (though may help convince a significant other), but can be useful in conveying your intentions to a contractor. Cross-sections, elevations and perspective drawings offer you scope to be creative – but there is no need to omit these on the basis that you think you can't draw. They can be kept very simple, even stylized (see the examples illustrated) and do not need to be particularly detailed. They merely give an impression (an 'artist's impression', literally). For instance, if you are drawing a wall, merely indicate a few of the bricks – for a dense planting, just sketch in a few of the flowers.

Cross-sections and elevations are particularly useful for conveying how you are planning to deal with a slope or uneven ground on the site or for indicating the relative heights of new fencing, screening or other planting. A cross-section is a slice through the garden in the vertical plane. Use your scale rule to ensure that proportions within the drawing are accurate. An elevation is similar but conveys a sense of depth, with a foreground and background. They can also be used to illustrate how a planting scheme will look (especially if you add colour). A couple of small cross-sections of the same part of the garden can indicate seasonal changes – perhaps to convey how a tree will look when in and out of leaf, or how herbaceous perennials will fill in a gap between permanent shrubs.

Francesca Certo

A cross-section can be used to convey the proportions of a new garden structure – in this case, a gazebo.

If you are not confident about drawing directly on the plan, create the image on a separate sheet (possibly of A4 or even A5, whatever you are comfortable with). If necessary, you can photocopy the image smaller or larger, then cut round it and stick it to the plan before copying the whole thing and adding colour.

To create a drawing to scale, lay a sheet of tracing paper over the plan and draw a straight line through the section you wish to 'elevate'. Mark on this line all the points that will appear in your drawing – edges of paths and borders, positions of trees, shrubs, hedges and fences, etc. Using the scale rule, reproduce the line, and the markings, to the appropriate scale for the drawing. Indicate the new scale to the side of the drawing. Note that if you scale up the measurements for drawing on a separate sheet then reduce this on a photocopier, you will effectively be using an intermediate scale. By comparing measurements between the plan and the reduced drawing (e.g. the width or a path or the distance between a tree trunk and border edge), it is possible to calculate what the new scale is.

Jackie Herald

Simple pencil sketches can be used to give a sense of what the new garden will look like.

Jackie Herald

Jackie Herald

A simple sketch on site can unlock your creativity.

If you think you don't have the necessary skills, a cheat's method is to find something similar to what you would like to draw in a book, magazine or trade catalogue. Trace whichever section you want onto tracing paper, then enlarge or shrink this using a photocopier. Add any extra detail as required (you can remove any unwanted lines with correction fluid). Photocopy this again to the appropriate size, cut round it, then paste it to your plan.*

This is a less technical, more conceptual approach – a scrupulous designer will annotate the sketch as 'not to scale'. But some sense of scale is usually implicit, if you are drawing a bench or some other familiar object is included. If the drawing includes a mature tree, you could indicate scale by incorporating a figure. It can, however, be useful to mark in the height of a proposed fence, pergola or wall, if this is to be added to the garden.

Adding colour to the drawing once you are satisfied with it can 'lift' the whole design. This does not have to be a slavish colouring-in exercise. A wash of green over the canopy of a stylized tree can be remarkably effective, and it is perfectly acceptable to leave some areas uncoloured.

*A hand drawing reduced in size on a photocopier looks remarkably professional.

MAKING A PERSPECTIVE DRAWING

A perspective drawing looks professional and is surprisingly easy to do, though the explanation sounds complicated. To create the drawing, it's necessary to begin with a grid in perspective.

To take the simplest example – imagine the garden is rectangular and ends in a wall (or solid fence or hedge). To the sides are also walls, fences or hedges (this 'shoebox' shape is actually fairly typical of many town gardens). As you stand with your back to the house (your 'standpoint'), you are confronted by the back wall in front of you (think of this as the 'picture frame'). The boundaries to either side recede from you, creating 'sight lines'. Imagine for a moment that these sight lines go on to a distant point where they converge (the 'vanishing point' – possibly at the other end of the universe, certainly some way outside the garden).

But the wall is real and can be measured. Measure from your standpoint to the wall, then select a point on it to act as the vanishing point – say around 2m above ground level. Draw the wall to a suitable scale on a separate sheet of paper. Mark on it the vanishing point that you selected. Choose a suitable scale for your grid (i.e. a number that will divide neatly into the width of the wall), then mark the base with a series of points – as if you were preparing to draw a conventional grid over the wall.

Scale down the distance of the standpoint to the vanishing point. Measuring from the vanishing point on the drawing, mark in a horizontal rule (either to the right or left) that equates to the distance from the standpoint. This will end in a point to one side of the wall.

From the vanishing point on the wall, draw a series of straight lines through the points at the base of the wall – these lines will radiate out in a fan shape. From the point to the side (that marks the standpoint) draw a second set of diagonals, also through the points along the base of the wall. In the area in front of the wall, draw a series of horizontal rules through the points where lines converge, parallel to the base of the wall and progressively longer. At some moment the 3D grid will leap out at you. Place a sheet of tracing paper over this and you will be able to use the grid as a guide for drawing simple objects in perspective.

You do not actually need a garden wall to create a grid. Just imagine some hypothetical huge mirror has been flung down into the garden and you are drawing what's reflected in it. The picture frame is in this case imaginary – its edges may be marked by a tree, the side of a shed, or nothing at all.

Information panel

This appears to the right of the plan and can be as detailed as you like. Use this space to list materials and plants.

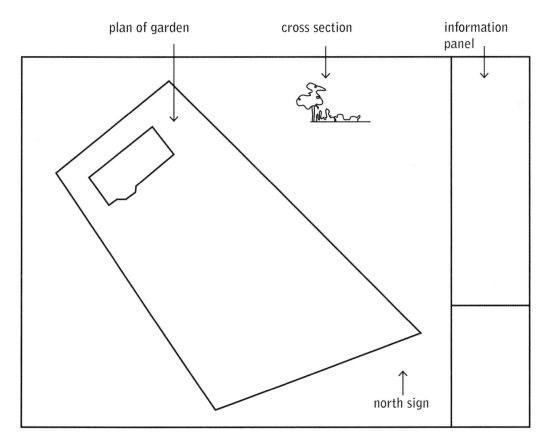

plan of garden   cross section   information panel

north sign

TITLE BLOCK

If you want your design to look really professional, add a title block beneath the information panel that includes the following information:

✓ Name of the designer and contact details
✓ Name of the client
✓ Title (e.g. 'development of back garden')
✓ Job number
✓ Scale
✓ Date
✓ Revisions*
✓ Drawn by**
✓ Date

COMPANY NAME AND LOGO		
CLIENT		
TITLE		
JOB NO.		SCALE
DATE	REV.	DRAWN BY
ANY OTHER INFORMATION		

Title block

*Use this to number successive draughts if changes need to be made to your first design. Leave this blank initially. If you need to go 'back to the drawing board', your next drawing (the first revision) can be numbered 1.

**Normally your own initials – unless (or until) you employ someone else to do this part of the job for you.

INDEX

Page numbers in *italics* indicate
an illustration